THE BOOKS OF ELIJAH
PARTS 1-2

Society of Biblical Literature

 TEXTS AND TRANSLATIONS
PSEUDEPIGRAPHA SERIES

edited by
Robert A. Kraft
Harold W. Attridge

Texts and Translations Number 18
Pseudepigrapha Number 8

*THE BOOKS OF ELIJAH
PARTS 1-2*
by
Michael E. Stone
and
John Strugnell

THE BOOKS OF ELIJAH
PARTS 1-2

collected and translated by
Michael E. Stone and
John Strugnell

comprehensive index by
W. Lowndes Lipscomb

Scholars Press

Distributed by
Scholars Press
PO Box 5207
Missoula, Montana 59806

THE BOOKS OF ELIJAH
PARTS 1-2
collected and translated by
Michael E. Stone
and
John Strugnell

Copyright © 1979
Society of Biblical Literature

Library of Congress Cataloging in Publication Data

The Books of Elijah.

(Pseudepigrapha series ; 8 ISSN 0145-3238)
(Texts and translations ; 18 ISSN 0145-3203)
Includes bibliographical references.
CONTENTS: Fragments of the Elijah literature,
collected and translated by M. E. Stone and
J. Strugnell.—The Vita Eliae, translated, together
with notes on The short history of Elijah the Prophet,
by M. E. Stone.—Comprehensive index, by
W. L. Lipscomb.
1. Elijah, the prophet. 2. Apocalyptic literature. I.
Stone, Michael E., 1938- II. Strugnell, John. III. Series.
IV. Series: Society of Biblical Literature. Texts and
translations ; 18.
BS580.E4B6   229'.913   79-15153
ISBN 0-89130-315-4
ISBN 0-89130-316-2 pbk.

Printed in the United States of America
1   2   3   4   5
Printing Department
University of Montana
Missoula, Montana 59812

PREFACE TO THE SERIES

TEXTS AND TRANSLATIONS is a project of the Committee on Research and Publications of the Society of Biblical Literature and is under the general direction of the Executive Secretary of the Society and the Chairman of the Committee. The purpose of the project is to make available in convenient and inexpensive format ancient texts which are not easily accessible but are of importance to scholars and students of "biblical literature" as broadly defined by the Society. Reliable modern English translations will accompany the texts. Occasionally the various series will include documents not published elsewhere. It is not a primary aim of these publications to provide authoritative new critical texts, nor to furnish extensive annotations. The editions are regarded as provisional, and individual volumes may be replaced in the future as better textual evidence becomes available. The following subseries have been established thus far:

> PSEUDEPIGRAPHA, edited by Robert A. Kraft (University of Pennsylvania) and Harold W. Attridge (Perkins School of Theology)

> GRECO-ROMAN RELIGION, edited by Hans Dieter Betz (University of Chicago)

> EARLY CHRISTIAN LITERATURE, edited by Birger A. Pearson (University of California at Santa Barbara)

For the PSEUDEPIGRAPHA SERIES the choice of texts is governed in part by the research interests of the SBL Pseudepigrapha Group, of which George W.E. Nickelsburg, Jr. (University of Iowa) is currently Chairman and James H. Charlesworth (Duke University), Secretary. This series will focus on Jewish materials from the Hellenistic era and will regularly include volumes that incorporate the fragmentary evidence of works attributed to biblical personalities, culled from a wide range of Jewish and Christian sources. The volumes are selected, prepared, and edited in consultation with the following editorial subcommittee of the Pseudepigrapha Group:

Sebastian P. Brock (Oxford, England)

George W. MacRae (Harvard Divinity School)

George W.E. Nickelsburg (University of Iowa)

Michael E. Stone (Hebrew University of Jerusalem)

John Strugnell (Harvard Divinity School)

Robert A. Kraft, Editor

Harold W. Attridge, Associate Editor

ACKNOWLEDGEMENTS

The preparation of this book has extended over a period of years and the editors are indebted to those who aided them in this task. W. Lowndes Lipscomb not only prepared the Index, but also spent much time in putting final touches on the camera-ready copy. Mary Walsh typed nearly all of the camera-ready copy with great patience and skill. Our gratitude is extended to both of them.

Robert A. Kraft and, later, Harold W. Attridge, gave us much counsel and assistance, both as colleagues and in their capicity as editors of <u>Texts and Translations</u>, <u>Pseudepigrapha Series</u>.

The cost of the typing of the camera-ready copy was borne by the University of Pennsylvania.

All citations from works under copyright are made with permission. The text of Bodleian Library, Ms. Heb. d.11, fols. 17v-r is published with the permission of the Keeper of Oriental Books, The Bodleian Library, Oxford. Biblical texts are cited from the R.S.V., adapted, where necessary, to the exigencies of the context.

Michael E. Stone
John Strugnell

CONTENTS

BOOKS OF ELIJAH

GENERAL PREFACE

This collection of Elianic texts and fragments represents a substantial portion of the writings attributed to this prophet that have survived. There are others, and the editors hope that, in the future, they will also be published in subsequent fasicles of Texts and Translations. Such works as the Sefer Eliyyahu, the Tanna deBe Eliyyahu and the Huppat Eliyyahu in Hebrew, the Gadle Elias in Ethiopic, and the Elijah texts of the various Christian hagiographic traditions, as well as certain fragments from Qumran Cave IV might well be included in such a sequel to the present volume.

It might be asked why the editors have seen fit to publish the present texts, among which few -- if indeed any -- can claim an antiquity comparable to the Apocrypha? The editors believe that, in antiquity there was at least one Elijah apocryphon. Certain features recur both in the surviving quotations and in the associated Coptic or Hebrew works, such as the physiognomic description of the Antichrist (1.11) or the description of Gehenna (1.1) where "the punishment fits the crime." These may well be indications of elements which were very early at home in the Elijah tradition. They need at least preliminary collection -- the task of analysis, of separation of precious metal from dross, lies further ahead.

The remarkably wide attestation of a saying such as "eye has not seen, nor ear heard . . ." (1.111) reminds one of the spread and influence of this material in byzantine, medieval and later literature. This dimension of the study of the pseudepigraphical literature too is important and all too often neglected. To investigate it will prove fruitful for the understanding of the way that these traditions worked in the development of Judaism and Christianity.

PART I

FRAGMENTS OF THE ELIJAH LITERATURE

INTRODUCTION

The first significant collection of Elianic legends is to be found, naturally, in C. Fabricius, Codex Pseudepigraphus Veteris Testamenti (2ed; Hamburg: Felginer, 1722) 1.1070-1086. He deals with our fragments nos. III and IV in Ch. CCVIII and with our Fg. VII in Ch. CCVII. Ch. CCIX discusses Hebrew exegetical tradition, as recorded in the Seder 'Olam Rabba (Ch. 17) and by Qimhi (on 2 Chron 21:12), about Elijah's disappearance, his expected return, and about the letter of Elijah brought (after his ascension) to King Joram (2 Chron 21:12).Ch. CCX records Carmelite, Persian Sufi, and other traditions on Elijah as founder of the hermit's way of life. Ch. CCXI discusses Christian beliefs about the return of Elijah (Malachi 4:5, cf. Matt 17:10, John 1:21, Rev 11:3, Justin Dial. 8:10, 49, Vitae Prophetarum sub nomine, Evang. Ps-Nicodemi 25), together with an analogous belief of the "Chymici" (e.g. Paracelsus) and his possible identity with Phineas (cf. also Bibl. Ant. 48 and H. Strack & P. Billerbeck, Kommentar z.N.T. 4.462P) and St. George (el-Ḥaḍr). Ch. CCXII discusses a rabbinical tradition of the "House of Elijah" or be Eliyyahu (attested in b. Aboda Zara' 9a, cf. b. Sanh 92a) that the world would last 6,000 years, and the survival of this tradition in Jewish-Christian polemic. It is not clear what is the floruit of this "House of Elijah". Ch. CCXIII mentions three Jewish Books attributed to Elijah, parts of which contain stories and speeches of the Prophet, the Seder Eliyyahu Rabba, the Seder Eliyyahu Zuta,[1] and

---

[1]Although a surviving Tanna debe Eliyyahu and a Seder Eliyyahu are mentioned in the Talmud (cf. b. Ket. 106a etc.), the present form of the surviving Tanna debe Eliyyahu (=Seder Eliyyahu Rabba + Seder Eliyyahu Zuta) is probably of late (i.e. ca. 9th century) date -- although it preserves the passages quoted by the Talmud. It may be consulted in the editions of Venice 1598 and of Vienna 1902, ed. M. Friedmann, as well as in H.M. Horowitz' Bibliotheca Haggadica 2.3-19; cf. Encyclopedia Judaica 15.803-804. Some would regard the work as being much older, while admitting later elements in it. A new English translation is currently under preparation.

the qnpt(?) 'lyhw (Cave of Elijah? non vidimus) -- Fabricius on
historical and linguistic grounds ascribes these to a younger
Elijah the Prophet, despite clear Hebrew tradition (b. Ket. 106a)
to the contrary! One might add to Fabricius' list of Hebrew works,
without being exhaustive, the Sa'arat Eliyyahu (ed. Wilna 1894)
and the Sefer Eliyyahu uPirqê Mašiaḥ (ed. A. Jellinek, Bet ha-
Midrasch 3.65-82).

More recently some of the fragments were gathered together in
English translation and discussed by M.R. James, Lost Apocrypha of
the Old Testament (London: S.P.C.K., 1920) 53-61; many of the Greek,
Latin, and Syriac texts were assembled in Michael E. Stone's
Apocryphal Fragments from Qumran and from the Church Fathers
(Jerusalem: Akademon, 1969) 29-38 [Hebrew]; the texts of our fgg.
II and III are also printed in Albert M. Denis, Fragmenta Pseude-
pigraphorum quae supersunt graeca (= Pseudepigrapha Veteris
Testamenti Graece III; Leiden: Brill, 1970) 103-4.

Bibliography on individual fragments will be given ad locc.
The existence of a recent discussion of the work, with abundant
references to current literature (A.M. Denis, Introduction aux
Pseudépigraphes Grecs d'Ancien Testament [Studia in Veteris testamenti Pseudepigrapha 1; Leiden: Brill, 1970] 163-9, 284, 298) spares
us from repeating here all the indications given there.

In this edition we only print fragments which may, as literary
pieces, go back to, or reflect knowledge of, an early Greek
apocryphal work on Elijah; of course many of the folkloristic and
midrashic traditions about Elijah (which in general concentrate on
his life, ascension, post-mortem appearances, and final return) may
also have occurred in (or perhaps even been derived from) this
work -- but there is no decisive evidence for this.

For the Elijah literature in general, cf. the bibliographical
indications in Theological Dictionary of the New Testament 3.928ff.,
s.v. ΗΛΕΙΑΣ (J. Jeremias); Bibliotheca Sanctorum 4.1022-1039,
s.v. Elia, profeta (T. Stramare, F. Spadafora, & F.M. Alfoldi);
F. Stegmuller, Repertorium Biblicum Medii Aevi I (Madrid: CSIC,
1940) nos. 90 and 120; E. Schürer, Geschichte des Jüdischen Volkes[3]..
(Leipzig: J.C. Hinrichs, 1909) 3.361-6

The Hebrew material is collected and/or discussed by J.D.
Eisenstein, Oṣar Midrashim I, pp. 24-26; M.W. Levinsohn, Der
Prophet Elias nach den Talmudim- und Midraschim-Quellen (N.Y.:
1929); R. Zion, Beiträge zur Geschichte und Legende des Propheten
Elia (Würzburg: 1931); L. Ginzberg, Legends of the Jews (Philadelphia: Jewish Publication Society, 1909-1938) 4.195-235, 6.316-
343, 7.133-135 (and consult also the sections there on Elisha),
and by [H.L. Strack and] P. Billerbeck, Kommentar zum Neuen Testament (München: Beck, 1926 ff.) 4.764-798.

For other possibly relevant traditions cf. A. Augustinovic,
"El-Khader" and the Prophet Elijah (Publications of the Studium
Biblicum Franciscanum, Collectio Minor 12; Jerusalem: Franciscan
Printing Press, 1972); Acta SS. Julii V. (Antwerp: Jacobus du
Moulin, 1727) 4-22; Elie le prophète(2 vols.; Bruges: 1956,non vidi).

The present collection does not pretend to advance our knowledge of these enigmatic fragments, but merely to gather them together in the best form in which scholarly endeavor has so far
presented them, and to make them readily available for the encour-
agement of further research.

Footnotes to each fragment occur following the text and
translation of it, and before the next fragment. The apparatuses
are adapted from the editions, in which indications of the
character and location of the manuscripts referred to can be found.

TITLES OF ELIANIC WRITINGS

<u>Title</u>:   the following forms are attested:

a) "The Secret/apocrypha (ἀπόκρυφον/-α) of Elijah." So Origen
(+ "the Prophet" cf. Fg III a T 1); Euthalius (Fg III a T 3);
George the Syncellus (Fg IV a T.4), quoted also by Zacharias
Chrysopolitanus, <u>Harmonia Evangelica</u> c. 166 (<u>Bibliotheca</u>
<u>Veterum Patrum</u>, 19.937); cf. "The Hidden Things (Apocrypha) of
Elijah" Mexit'ar of Ayrivank', Erevan MS. no. 1500, p. 370, in
Stone, "Canon Lists III," <u>HTR</u> 69 (1976) 289-300.

b) "The Apocrypha said to be of the Prophet Elijah." So Photius,
<u>ad Amphilochum</u> Qn 151 (Fg III a T 3b.).

c) "The Apocalypse of Elijah among the Apocrypha (<u>in apocalypsi</u>
<u>Heliae in apocryphis</u>)." So Ambrosiaster (Fg III a T 2),
(<u>apocalypsis H.</u>);Jerome (Fg III a T 6-7); Pseudo-Anastasius
Sinaita, <u>List of 60 Books</u>; Slavonic Versions of the <u>List of</u>
<u>60 Books</u> (Denis, <u>Introduction</u>, xii).

d) "The Prophecy (<u>prophetia</u>) of Elijah." So Anastasius Biblio-
thecarius' Latin version of Nicephorus' Stichometry, Fabricius,
<u>Cod. Pseud</u>. 1, 1074.

e) "Of Elijah the Prophet." So Pseudo-Athanasius, <u>Synopsis</u>;
Nicephorus, <u>Stichometry</u> (+ "of 3016 [or 316] verses);
<u>Chronographia Compendiaria</u>.

f) "Apocryphal Books (βιβλία ἀπόκρυφα) of Elijah." So <u>Apostolic</u>
<u>Constitutions</u> 6, 16, 3.

g) "Elijah." So Epiphanius (Fg IV a T 1).

h) "Of a Prophet." So Maximus (pseudo-Ambrose).

i) "The Apocryphon of Jeremiah." So George the Syncellus (Fg
IV a T 2).

We should certainly distinguish from this the title once given
to Eupolemus' work, "a work about the prophecy of Elijah" [ἔν τινι
περὶ τῆς Ἡλίου προφητείας]   cited <u>via</u> Alexander Polyhistor by
Eusebius, <u>Praep</u>. <u>Evangelica</u> IX.30.; cf. the discussion in B.Z.
Wacholder, <u>Eupolemus: a Study of Judaeo-Greek Literature</u> (Mono-
graphs of the Hebrew Union College III; Cincinnati-New York: Hebrew
Union College - Jewish Institute of Religion, 1974) 21-24.

Fragment I

THE TORMENTS OF THE DAMNED

14

Fragment I. The Torments of the Damned.[1]

Ia.   In the Epistula Titi discipuli Pauli de dispositione sanctimonii, we find the following quotation:

Furthermore the Prophet Elijah bears witness that he had a

vision. "The angel of the Lord", he says, "showed me a deep

valley, which is called Gehenna, burning with sulphur and

pitch, and in that place are many souls of sinners, and there

they are tormented with various tortures. Some suffer in

hanging by their genitals, others by their tongues, some by

their eyes, others in hanging upside down. Women will be

tortured in their breasts, and young men by hanging by their

hands. Some virgins are burnt on a gridiron, and other souls

are pierced by an unceasing torment. By these various tortures

the acts of each are shown forth. Adulterers and pederasts

are tortured in their genitals. Those who hang by their

tongues are the blasphemers and false witnesses. Those who

hang by their eyes (or "have their eyes burnt") are those who

have stumbled through their glances and who have looked with

craving on guilty acts. Those hanging upside down are those

who hate God's righteousness, men of evil minds, none of whom

is in harmony with his brother. Deservedly then are they

burned (?) according to· the punishment to which they are sen-

tenced. As for the fact that women are sentenced to be

punished by tortures in their breasts, these are women who las-

civiously have **yielded** their bodies to men: and their men will

be nearby in tortures, hanging by their hands for this reason."

[Ep. Titi, lines 400-417; cf. Hennecke-Schneemelcher 2.158]

400 Denique testatur propheta Helias uidisse: Ostendit, inquid,

mihi angelus domini conuallem altam quae uocatur gehenna ar-

densque sculphore et bitumine. Et in illo loco sunt multae

animae peccatorum et taliter ibi cruciantur diuersis tormentis:

paciuntur aliqui pendentes natura[e], alii autem linguis,/

405 quidam uero oculis, alii inuersi pendentes, et foemine mam-

millis suis cruciabuntur, et iuuenes manibus pendentes, quae-

dam in craticula uirgines uruntur et quaedam figuntur animae

perpetuae poenae. Per ipsa uero uaria supplicia ostenditur

uniuscuiusque actus: naturalium †dolor utique†adulteri sunt

410 et pederasti; qui/autem linguis suspenduntur blasphemi sunt,

falsi etiam testes; qui oculis uero cremantur hii sunt qui in

adtend<end> o scandalizati sunt respicientes in concupiscencia

reatu gesta; qui uero inuersi pendebant hii sunt odientes

iusticiam dei, praui consilii, nec quisquam fratri consentit,

415 merito ergo poenis sentenciae uruntur;/nam quod foeminae mam-

millis torqueri iubentur istae sunt quae in ludibrio corpus

suum tradiderunt masculis, ideoque et ipsi iuxta erunt in

tormentis manibus pendentes p<ropt>er hanc rem.

406 quidem in Raticlam MS   409 pederasti MS^{m1}? : perditi^{m2}
411 adtend<end>o: adtendo MS: videndo de Bruyne   414 ergo de
Bruyne: et in MS   415 torquere MS   415 qui MS   417 p<ropt>er
de Bruyne : per? MS

Epistula Titi discipuli Pauli de dispositione sanctimonii, ed. D.
de Bruyne, Rev. Ben. 37 (1925) 58

1b i. An analogous Hebrew text, also related to Elijah, is found in the Chronicles of Jerahmeel XIV.4. We cite the text of the unique MS of Jerahmeel (Bodleian MS. Hebr. d 11, p. 17), as it is transcribed by M.E. Stone, op. cit. (Introduction, supra) 36-7. Our translation is modified from that of M. Gaster, The Chronicles of Jerahmeel (Oriental Translation Fund NS 4; London: Royal Asiatic Society, 1898) 34-5; cf. now pp. 30-31 of the Introduction to the Ktav reprint, NY: 1972. Gaster's additional material is apparently drawn from diverse sources not indicated in detail by him. One such is Reshith Hokhmah of Elia de Vida, the text of the relevant portion of which has been given below (I b ii). This section of Reshith Hokhmah was also reprinted by Jellinek, Bet ha-Midrasch I,

1   R. Joshua[3-4] said. "Once upon a time I was walking on my way, and I found Elijah --[5]may his memory be for blessing[5]. He said to me 'Do you want me to make you stand near the gate of Gehenna?' and I said to him 'Yes'. Then he showed me men [6]hanging by their hands and men hanging by their tongues and men hanging by their eyes and men hanging by their ears[6].

2   And he showed me men who were made to eat fiery coals [7]and men who were sitting and alive, while worms were eating them[7].

3   And he showed me men who were made to eat fine sand: they were made to eat it against their will, and their teeth were broken by the sand. And the Holy One blessed be He says to them '[8]You ate things that you stole [9]in this world[9], and they were sweet in your mouth; but now you do not have the strength to

147-149. Further expansions of the Jerahmeel translation are given below in the form of footnotes to the English translation of I b i. The Hebrew for them was not available.

A further extensive reworking of this material, formulated as a revelation to Moses by the Prince of Gehenna, is to be found in the late Moses apocryphon, Gedulat Moshe (ed. Amsterdam: 1753) fols. 5r-7r. This may also have served Gaster as one of the sources for his expansions.

1 אמר ר' יהושע פעם אחת הייתי מהלך בדרך ומצאתי אליהו ז"ל ואמר
לי: רצונך שאעמידך על שער גהינום, ואמרתי לו: הן. והראני בני
אדם שתלויין בידיהם ובני אדם שתלויין בלשונם ובני אדם שתלויין
בעיניהם ובני אדם שתלויין באזניהם.

2 והראני בני אדם שמאכילין אותם גחלי רתמים ובני אדם שיושבים
וחיים ותולעים אוכלים אותם.

3 והראני בני אדם שמאכילים אותם חול דק והיו מאכילין אותם בעל כרחם
ושיניהם משתברין מן החול. והקב"ה אומר להם: אתם אכלתם את הגזל
בעולם הזה והיה מתוק בפיכם. עתה אין בכם כוח לאכול לקיים מה
שנאמר: ושיני רשעים שיברתי.

eat' -- to confirm what is said '[10]I have[10] broken the teeth
of the wicked.'" (Ps 3:8)[11]

Ib ii. Another version of this text is that to be found in Reshith
Hokhmah (see I b i above). This contains extensive additional material to that in the Jerahmeel text. This additional material is
underlined in the following translation.

1   Rabbi Joshua ben Levi said, "Once upon a time I was walking on
    my way and Elijah the prophet -- may his memory be for a bless-
    ing -- found me. He said to me, 'Do you want me to make you
    stand near the gate of Gehenna?' I said to him, 'Yes.' He
    showed me men hanging by their noses and men hanging by their
    hands and men hanging by their tongues and men hanging by
    their feet; and he showed me women hanging by their breasts,
    and he showed me men hanging by their eyes.

2   And he showed me men who were made to eat their own flesh,
    and men who were made to eat fiery coals, and men who were
    sitting alive while worms were eating them. He said to me,
    'These are those of whom it is written (Isa 66:24): Their worm
    shall not die.'"

3   (Identical, except for minor variations, with the text of
    Jerahmeel.)

4   And he showed me men who were being cast from the fire to
    snow and from the snow to fire, like this shepherd who pas-
    tures his sheep from mountain to mountain, concerning whom
    scripture says (Ps 49:14): Like sheep they are appointed for
    Sheol: Death shall be their shepherd; And the upright shall
    have dominion over them in the morning; And their form shall

1 אמר ר׳ יהושע בן לוי פעם אחת הייתי מהלך בדרך ומצאני אליהו
הנביא זכור לטוב, אמר לי: רצונך שאעמידך על שער גהינם. אמרתי
לו: הן. הראני בני אדם שתלויים בחוטמיהם, ובני אדם שתלויים
בידיהם, ובני אדם שתלויים בלשונותם, ובני אדם שתלויים ברגליהם,
והראני נשים תלויות בדדיהן, והראני בני אדם שתלויים בעיניהם.

2 והראני בני אדם שמאכילים אותם
בשרם, ובני אדם שמאכילים אותם גחלי רתמים, ובני אדם יושבים
חיים ותולעים אוכלים אותם. אמר לי: אלו שכתוב עליהם כי תולעתם
לא תמות.

3 (זהה עם נוסח ירחמיאל, להוציא כמה שנויים קלים).

4 והראני בני אדם שמשליכין אותם מן האש לשלג ומן השלג לאש כרועה
זה שרועה את צאנו מהר להר, ועליהם הכתוב אומר: כצאן לשאול שתו
מות ירעם וירדו בם ישרים לבקר וצורם (קי) לבלות שאול מזבל לו.

be for Sheol to wear away, that there be no habitation for
it.

Ic. Another analogous passage occurs in J̲era̲h̲meel XVI:1-5 (Bodleian MS Heb. d 11, p. 17), this time associated with the prophet
Isaiah. Again we cite the text of the MS as given by Stone, op.
cit. ('Introduction' supra) 37-8; additional material in Gaster's
translation, op. cit.(supra, Ib i) 36-7, is given in footnotes to
the translation; its Hebrew text is found in Jellinek, Bet ha-
Midrasch 5.50-51.

1   There are five law courts (?) established in Gehenna, and
    Isaiah the son of Amoz saw them all. He entered the first
    court, and saw, and behold[12] men carrying buckets of water
    on their shoulders, and they kept filling them and emptying
    them into a well, but the well never fills [13]and the men
    never die[13]. He (Isaiah) said to Him (God),"[14]Reveal the
    mystery[14], O Revealer of Mysteries, explain to me the vision."
    And the [15]Holy Spirit answered and said to him "These are the
    men who coveted what was not theirs while they were in the
    world, and transgressed against what is written in the Torah
    'You shall not covet.' (Exod 20:17) Now they are brought here
    and judged here."[15]

2   He entered the second court and he saw there[16] men hanging by
    their tongues; and he said to him "O Revealer of Mysteries, ex-
    plain the vision to me." [17]The Holy Spirit[17] answered him "These
    are the men who [18]slandered their companions while they were
    in the world, and transgressed what is written in the Torah
    'You shalt not go up and down as a slanderer among your people'
    (Lev 19:16). And now they are brought here and judged here."[18]

[ספר ראשית חכמה, קושטאנדינה, דף מ' עמ. א']

1   חמישה בתי דינין קבועים בגהינום וכולם ראה אותם ישעיהו בן אמוץ.
נכנס לבית הראשון וראה הנה בני אדם שאוחזים כדי מים על שכמיהם
וממלאין ומשליכין לתוך הבאר והבאר אינו מתמלא, ובני אדם אינן
מתין.אמר לפניו: גלא רז, גלא רזים פרוש לי החזון.   השיבה אותו
רוח הקודש ואמרה לו: אלו בני אדם שחומדים דבר שאינו שלהם בהיותם
בעולם ועוברין על מה שכתוב בתורה: לא תחמוד, עכשיו מביאין אותן
כאן ודנין אותם כאן.

2   נכנס לבית השני וראה שם בני אדם תלויין בלשונן: ואמר לפניו
גלא רזיא פרוש לי החזון.   השיבה אותו רוח הקודש: אלו בני האדם
שאכלו קורציהם דחבריהון בהיותם בעולם ועברו על מה שכתוב בתורה:
לא תלך רכיל בעמך.   ועכשיו מביאין אותם כאן ודנין אותן בכך.

3 He entered the third court, and saw[19] men hanging by their testicles. He said to Him "O Revealer of Mysteries, explain to me the vision."[20] The Holy Spirit answered him and said to him "These are the men who were in the world and afflicted the daughters of Israel (?), who are compared to a calf -- as it is said 'Ephraim was a trained heifer' (Hos 10:11) -- and walked after the daughters of the uncircumcised, who are compared to asses -- as it is said 'whose flesh is that of asses' (Ezek 23:20) -- and now they are brought here and judged **thus** ."[20]

4 He entered the fourth court, and saw there [21]daughters of iniquity[21] hanging by the nipples of their breasts; and he said to Him "O Revealer of Mysteries, explain to me the vision." [22]The Holy Spirit answered him and said to him[22] "These[23] are the women who uncovered their hair and rent their veil and sat in the open market place to suckle their children, in order to attract the gaze of men and to make them sin; therefore they are punished thus."

5 He entered the fifth court, and found it full of smoke. There were all the governors, the chiefs, and Pharaoh the wicked presiding over them and watching over the gate of hell, and he says to them,"Why did you not learn from me when I was in Egypt?" Thus he sits there and watches at the gatehouse of hell.[24]

3 נכנס לבית השלישי וראה בני אדם תלויין בעגבותיהם, אמר לפניו:
גלא רזיא פרוש לי החזון . השיבה אותו רוח הקודש ואמרה לו:
אלו בני אדם שהיו בעולם שהיו מציקין בנות ישר(אל?) שמשילות
לעגלה שנאמר: אפרים עגלה מלומדה והולכין אחר בנות ערלים
שמשילות לחמורים שנאמר: אשר בשר חמורים בשרם, ומביאין אותם
לכאן ודנין אותם בכך.

4 נכנס לבית הרביעי וראה שם בנות הרשעה שתלויות בחוטי דדיהן ואמר
לפניו: גלא רזיא פרוש לי החזון . השיבה אותו רוח הקוש אמרה לו:
אלו הנשים אשר גילו את שערן וקרעו את צעיפן וישבו בשוק להיניק
את ילדיהן כדי למשוך את מבטי האנשים ולהביא אותם לידי חטא.
לכן . הן נענשות כך.

5 נכנס לבית החמישי ומצא אותו מלא עשן , שם היו כל השרים והנשיאים
ופרעה הרשע יושב בראשם ושומר את שער גהינום, והוא אומר אליהם:
למה לא למדתם ממני כשהייתי במצרים? כך הוא יושב ושומר בית שער
גהינום.

Older analogous Hebrew and Aramaic texts are discussed by S. Lieber-
mann, "On Sins and their Punishment," Louis Ginzberg Jubilee Volume
(New York: Amer. Acad. Jew. Res., 1945) 2.249-267 [Hebrew]. There
he prints our Fg.Ia, with a Hebrew translation. The oldest of
these Hebrew and Aramaic texts is that of a Geniza fragment published by L. Ginzberg, Geniza Studies (New York: J.T.S., 1928)
1.196f. [Hebrew]. That is ascribed to Tanna deBe Eliyyahu, but
it does not occur in the manuscript or the printings of that work.

1.   Note the connection of these fragments with the Hebrew <u>Sefer</u>
<u>Eliyyahu</u> (ed. Buttenwieser) 15, especially "again (the) Spirit
lifted me up and carried me to the west (end) of the world: and
I saw there souls suffering judgement in agony, each one according to his deeds." That work also contains a description of the
Antichrist, cf. fg II infra.

2.   For more recent discussions, cf. A. de Santos Otero, in E.
Hennecke - W. Schneemelcher, <u>New Testament Apocrypha</u> (Philadelphia:
Lutterworth Press and Westminster Press, 1965) 2.141-3 and 158 n.1.
Our translation is modified from that of de Santos Otero, ibid.
The sole MS of the Epistle (MS Th f28 of Würzburg University) is
of the eighth century; the date and place of composition are un-
certain; it is not even certain whether the Letter was translated
from Greek or composed in Latin, although the former seems likely.

3-4.   + Son of Levi: Re$\check{s}$ith Ḥokhma (RH).

5.   + the prophet: RH.

6-6.   hanging by their hair (noses: RH); and he said to me, 'These
were the men that let their hair grow to adorn themselves for sin.'
Others were hanging by their eyes; these were they that followed
their eyes to sin, and did not set God before them. Others were
hanging by their noses; these were they that perfumed themselves
to sin. Others were hanging by their tongues; these were they
that had slandered. Others were hanging by their hands; these
were they that had stolen and robbed. Others were hanging by their
sexual organs (<u>or</u> ignominiously); these were they that had committed
adultery. Others were hanging by their feet; these were they that
had run to sin. He showed me women hanging by their breasts; these
were they that uncovered their breasts before men, to make them
sin: Gaster.

7.   + these were they who had blasphemed. Others were forced to
eat bitter gall; these were they that ate on fast-days: Gaster.

8.   + O ye sinners: Gaster.

9-9.   + and robbed: Gaster.

10-10.   Thou hast: Gaster.

11.   Thus far the text parallel with the quotation in the Epistle
to Titus. Jeraḥmeel continues his apparently Elianic material as
follows (but Stone <u>op</u>. <u>cit</u>. does not give the Hebrew text, and we
translate according to the text of 'Orḥot Ḥayyim): 4 He showed me
further men who are thrown from fire to fire, and from snow to fire;
these were they that abused the poor who came to them for assistance; therefore are they thus punished, as it is said, "Thou didst

26

let men ride over our heads; we went through fire and through water"
(Ps 66:12). He showed me others who were driven from mountain to
mountain, as a shepherd leads the flock from one mountain to another. Of these speaks the verse: "Like sheep they are appointed
for Sheol; Death shall be their shepherd; and the upright shall
have dominion over them in the morning, and their form shall be
for Sheol to wear away, that there be no habitation for it" (Ps 49:
14). This may be a preferable form of the text printed under II.4.

12.   + two: Gaster.

13-13.   om. : Gaster.

14-14.   om. : Gaster.

15-15.   Spirit of the Lord answered, "These are the men who coveted
the property of their neighbors, and this is their punishment.":
Gaster.

16. + two: Gaster.

17-17.   He: Gaster.

18-18.   slandered, therefore they are thus punished: Gaster.

19.   + there: Gaster.

20-20.   And he answered "These are the men who neglected their
own wives, and committed adultery with the daughters of Israel.":
Gaster.

21-21.   women: Gaster.

22-22.   And he answered: Gaster.

23.   Henceforth we cite Gaster's translation, the MS being defec-
tive.

24.   The text continues with a description of the seven compart-
ments of hell -- which seems to have no relationship either to the
pericope we have printed or to the text of Fg. Ia.

Fragment II

THE APPEARANCE OF THE ANTICHRIST

Fragment II.   The Appearance of the Antichrist.

A physiognomic description of the Antichrist, attributed to Elijah, is found in one Greek MS (cf. Fg.IIa below).   This description recurs in various forms in another eleven works.   For a better
understanding of the text and its traditions we have appended a
diagram indicating in parallel columns the variations between these
witnesses.   The diagram sets the features forth in the order in
which they occur in the texts.

IIa (cf. Col. 1).   This is the only form of the text containing
an attribution to Elijah.   We print the text of Parisinus
Graecus 4, fol. 228r.   The text was first printed by F. Nau,
Journal Asiatique XI.9 (1917) 454;   we have regularized the
orthography.

IIb (cf. Col. 2).   This Syriac text, part of the Testamentum
Domini nostri J.C., derives from pp. 14-15 of Ign. Ephraim II
Rahmani's edition (Moguntiae:1899).   Rahmani gives the text of
3 MSS, Mossulanus of AD 1651/2 (=M), Borgianus 148 of AD 1576
(=B), and Sangermanensis 38 of sec. VIII [= Par. Syr. 62]
(=S); he refers on his p. xii to another Borgianus, with an
Arabic text derived from Coptic, but he seems never to have
published this. A. Baumstark, Geschichte der Syrischen Litter-
atur (Bonn: A. Marcus und E. Webers Verlag, 1922) 252 (notes
3 and 7) and 353, lists other MSS and recensions of this work
(which formed part of the Clementine Octateuch of the Syrian
Church, a work distinct from the Apostolic Constitutions) together with other partial editions and discussions.

'Εμφέρεται ἐν ἀποκρύφοις ὅτι 'Ηλίας ὁ προφήτης εἶπε περὶ τοῦ
'Αντιχρίστου· οἶος μέλλη τότε φαίνεσθαι· ἡ κεφαλὴ αὐτοῦ φλὸξ
πυρός· ὁ ὀφθαλμὸς αὐτοῦ ὁ δεξιὸς κέκραται αἵματος· ὁ δὲ
εὐώνυμος χαροπὸς ἔχων δύο κόρας· τὰ δὲ βλέφ[αρα] αὐτοῦ λευκά,
τὸ δὲ χεῖλος αὐτοῦ τὸ κάτω μέγα· ὁ δεξιὸς αὐτοῦ μηρὸς λεπτός,
καὶ οἱ πόδες αὐτοῦ πλατεῖς, τέθλασται δὲ ὁ μέγας δάκτυλος
τοῦ ποδὸς αὐτοῦ.

λεπτός] MS   λευκός

1. Titulus ܝܠ܇ ܙ ܝ ܒ ܒ ܐ ܕ ܕ ܐ܇ ܘ ܠ ܚ ܗ ܘܕ ܘ ܘ ܠ ܚ ܘ ܕ ܝ ܠ ܐ ܬ ܕ ܝ ܠ ܘ
ܪ ܘ ܡ ܠ ܐ ܝ   S   ܐ ܠ ܡ ܝ ܠ   2   ܝ ܡ ܗ ܕ ܐ ܚ ܝ ܕ ܡ ܝ ܡ ܝ ܠ   M B
3   ܘ ܠ ܚ ܗ   S   4 MB om this clause

IIc (cf. Col. 3). This is part of a long quotation of the
Testamentum Domini nostri JC described as being from the text
of "Clement," i.e. the Clementine Octateuch, made by Mos̆e b.
Kēpha in a homily on the advent of the Antichrist [on this
work cf. A. Baumstark, op. cit., p. 282, notes 4-10]. Our
text derives from C = Cambr. Add 2918 of AD 1218, [printed
by J.P. Arendzen, JTS 2 (1900-1) 410], P 206 = Parisinus Syr.
206 fol. 126 r-v and P. 207 = Parisinus Syr. 207 fol. 240
[printed by F. Nau, Journal Asiatique IX.17 (1901) 233 ff.].

IId (cf. Col. 4). The text is that of Codex Trevirensis 36
fol.113 (AD 719) reprinted from M.R. James, Apocrypha Anecdota
I, (Texts and Studies II.3; Cambridge; Camb. U.P., 1893)
152-7, cf. 187-8. The MS contained S. Prosper of Aquitaine's
de promissionibus et praedictionibus, and then two concluding
"fillers", this text (as part of a quotation giving ch. XI,
VI - VIII of the Testamentum Domini) and some Versus Sibyllae
beginning Veniet enim Rex omnipotens et aeternus.

IIe (cf. Col. 5). This text is taken from the edition of the
Testament in Galilee of our Lord J.C. by L. Guerrier and S.
Grébaut (Patrologia Orientalis 9.3; Paris: Firmin-Didot, 1912)
183, an edition based on 4 Ethiopic MSS, L = Brit. Mus. Or.
793 (sec. XVIII), A = Paris, Bib. Nat. Fonds d'Abbadie N⁰ 51
("écriture ancienne"), B = Paris Bib. Nat. Fonds d'Abbadie 90
("écriture guilḥ ancienne"), C = Paris Bib. Nat. Fonds d'Abbadie

حـ ف محللـا مخـالـا حـ (حبـا) هٰـٓ : مكـم (ـم (حبـا) اللاقضحي ١١٦ٓاا ٠٠٥٠.مٔ حـ حـا محما حكقل مخمط. ٥١ه.١مٔ مكمقلـ
مممهٔ هـممهٔ، (اللحمل (ـلـ حـا حٔقـل حـقحٔ (حنتحي ١حٔاه١٥. لـٔهٔضع مممقٔهٔ.
ممهٔ مـهمـ (لـلـلـ مـمٔـمٔ (خـلـ مٔ حـا حٔ هـٔ حـحنٔ مممطـٔ (حملـ (محٔ مخنـٔ خمنـٓ (حذٔ) (حٔا م حـلـا ٣ (حٔخٔ) حٔا هـممـ مٔ محننخيـ
حٔا ٥ هـ هـمـ (حللنخ.

Hec sunt signa Antichristi: Caput eius sicut flamma ignis, oculi eius

fellini: sed dexter sanguine mixtus erit, sinister autem glaucus[1] et

duos pupulos habens: supercilia uero alba, labium inferiorem maior-

em, dextrum femur eius macrum, tibie tenues, pedes lati, fractus

erit maior digitus eius: Iste est falx desolationis[2] et multis quasi

christus adstabit.

1 <u>cod.</u> gaudens.   2 fallax dilectionis <u>cod.</u>

ወእሊሁ፡ በእስራጠ፡ የዐይ፡ ግበር፡ ወበጋጦሙ፡ ጸሐዐት፡
ወዘወእኩ፡ ተእዎሬቱ፡ ርእኪ፡ ነጠ፡ ነደ፡ እሳፍ ፡፡ ዐዒሁ፡
የዐባይ፡ ፍሩሕ፡ ለጸም፡ ወዖ ጋዐዋ፡ ግዐሙ ፡፡ ጸሐኩወግ፡
ሐገፍ፡ ግደጋ፡ ዐዳይ፡ በመ.ሐፍ! ቀሪገለቱሁ፡ ታሐፈ ዋ፡
ግገሬረ፡ የዐዚ ፡፡ እገ ለሁ፡ ጸፈጸፍ፡ ወእጋግነ፡ ዐዐገ ዛግ
ዒቱሁ፡ ዘእገዴ፡[2] ጸገጸዋፍ፡ ዛወእኩ፡ ዐየበጸ፡ ወሐነ፡

199, and 795 = Brit. Mus. Or. 795 (sec. XVIII). Useful material can also be found in I.Wajnberg apud C. Schmidt, Gespräche Jesu mit seinen Jüngern (Texte und Untersuchungen 43; Leipzig: J.C. Hinrichs, 1919) 61*-62*, which adds a collation of S = Stuttgart Cod. Or. fol. N 49.

IIf (cf. Col. 6). The text is that of the Ethiopic version of the Tiburtine Sibyl, taken from J. Schleifer, "Die Erzählung der Sibylle, ein Apokryph," K. Ak. Wiss. Wien. Phil-Hist. Kl. Denkschriften 53 (Wien: 1910) 44-45, 70 (cf. also R. Basset, Les Apocryphes Ethiopiens X [Paris: Bibliothèque de la Haute Science, 1900] 36). It should be noted that the Latin and Greek forms of the Tiburtine Sibyl (for the former cf. J. Schleifer, op. cit. and for the latter cf. P.J. Alexander, The Oracle of Baalbek [Dumbarton Oaks Studies 10; Washington: Dumbarton Oaks, 1967])do not have this text in their variant accounts of the eschaton.

IIg (cf. Col. 7). An Arabic version of the Tiburtine Sibyl: the text is from J. Schleifer, op. cit. 45, 70.

IIh (cf. Col. 8). The Garshuni text of the Wisdom of the Sibyl is from J. Schleifer, op. cit. 44, 70.

1 በውኅት፡] AC ወአገት፡ LB
2 ኡጽዋሬ፦] om A

ወትኧዎዐሬ፡ [1] ሎውኧት፡ በኧሕ፡ በያዬ፡ር ኧሕ፡ ወቀጠኝ፡
ኻሕኚ፡ ወውትኚ፡ ሡዐሬት፡ ርኧሕ፡ ወያዬኝ፡ ወኧዪዐት፡ [2]
ወትዪሬት፡ ኧዪበዒሁ፡ [3] ወያዐዪዬ፡ ዐዪሬ፡ [4] ቱሕሕ፡
በዪዎ፡ ወበጋዐዪ፡ ዐዪሬ፡ ቱውኧ፡ [5]

[1] A1 ወነዐዒ፡ ቱዪዎሬ፡ (sic)   [2] D W Z2
ይዒቱ፡ ወዪዪዐት፡ A2 Z1 ወዪቀሕት፡ ወዪሱዐት፡
[3] A2 W Z2 ወትዪሬር ኧዪበዒሁ፡ A1 ወትዪሬር
ኧዪበኧት፡ Z1 ወትዪዬት፡ ኧዪበዒሁ፡ [4] W Z2 ወዪዐዪ፡
ዐዪሕ፡ and om ቱሕሕ፡ በዪዎ፡ ወበጋዐዪ፡ ዐዪሬ፡
[5] A2 ቱውኧ፡ Z1 ቱሕሕ፡ A1 om

وصفة هذا الرجل يكون رقيق الرقبة طويل الذراعين[1]
قصير الأصابع وعينيه لها نور كنور الشمس وفي عينه[2]
اليمين علامه

الذارعين 1Ms.   2 Ms. عينية

ويطلب[1] هوا الله صفى دائب[2] با[3] الإجز م[4] سه شحذ الذاه
بجلي الصمف لهملا الديؤاحي[2] حلؤ الإؤاحد حسه الصمفسة
اؤ ما صهب

1 om O   2 P الياؤحي   3 P ؤحد P 4؟
4 P الصمف

11i (cf. Col. 9). Cf. R. Basset, op. cit. 51-2. Bib. Nat.
Fonds Arabe 70.

11j (cf. Col. 10). Cf. R. Basset, op. cit. 61. The text is
that of Paris, B.N. Fonds Arabe 281.

11k (Col. 11). The text is that of the Ethiopic Baruch, as
found in the Falasha MS edited by J. Halévy, "Te'ězâza Sanbat"
(Commandements du Sabat) accompagné de six autres écrits
pseudo-épigraphiques admis par les Falachas ou Juifs
d'Abyssinie (Bibliothèque de l'Ecole des Hautes Etudes:
Sciences historiques et philologiques 137; Paris: E. Bouillon,
1902) 95 (text), 208 (translation). For an English translation with notes, see Wolf Leslau, Falasha Anthology (Yale
Judaica Series 4; New Haven: Yale U.P., 1951) 75-76.

11l (Col. 12) gives an Ethiopic text related to that of Col.
11. This is appended to the Ethiopic Sybil. In fact, the
whole "Appendix" to that work gives the Christian form of the
Apocalypse which concludes the Falasha Baruch (see 11k); from
J. Schleifer, op. cit. (cf. supra, on Col. 6) 78-9.

وصفة هذا الرجل كبير الراس رقيق الرقبه جيد
الشعر طويل الذراعين قصير الاصابع عيناه سرج
كنور الشمس وفي عينه¹ اليسرى نكته
عينيه ¹S,

وصفة هذا الرجل الذي هو المسيح الدجال كبير الراس رقيق
الرقبه طويل الذراعين قصير الاصابع¹ وعيناه لها نور كضو
الشمس وفي عينه اليمنى كيفيه

1 قصير الاصابع perhaps corrupt from
حلق الاواحد (11h) so also 11g,i

ወይ ዐግ ኘ ደ፡ ኛ ደ ኢ፡ ተ ሕ ሕ፡ በ ደ ም፡
ኧ ግ ሬ፡ ዘ ይ ዐ ግ ኝ፡ ቀ ጢ ግ፡ ወ ጽ ፉ ሬ፡ ኧ ደ ዒ ሁ፡
ጽ ን ጽ ዋ ት፡ ጽ ፉ ሬ፡ ኧ ደ ዒ ሁ፡ ወ ኧ ግ ሬ ሁ፡
ክ ሠ ወ፡ ማ ዕ ዐ ደ፡ ይ ዐ ግ ኢ፡ ለ ኧ ተ ፉ ኧ፡ ወ ደ ኃ ም ዉ፡
ለ ም ት፡

ይ ዐ ግ ኝ፡ ዐ ደ ኢ፡ በ ደ ም፡ ፎ ሕ ሕ፡ ወ ኧ ግ ሬ፡
ዘ ይ ዐ ግ ግ፡ ቀ ጢ ግ፡ ወ ጽ ፉ ሬ፡ ኧ ደ ዒ ሁ፡ ጽ ን ጽ ዋ ት፡
ወ ኧ ግ ሬ ሁ፡ ማ ዕ ዐ ደ፡ ደ ዐ ግ ኢ፡ ለ ኧ ሕ ፉ ጠ፡
ወ ደ ጋ ም ዉ፡ ም ት፡

	IIa Paris Gr 4 fol 288r	IIb Syriac Test. Dom. a	IIc Syriac Test. Dom. b	IId Cod.Treverensis 36 fol 113	IIe Ethiopic Test. Dom. in Gal.	IIf Ethiopic Tib. Sibyl	IIg Arabic Sibyl	IIh Garshuni Sibyl	IIi Arabic Tib. Sibyl	IIj Arabic Tib. Sibyl	IIk Falasha Baruch	III Ethiopic Wisdom Sibyl
Head: flame of fire	x											
large		x	x	x	x							
Neck: narrow						x	x	x	x			
Hairs:						few		thick	plentiful	x		
Arms: long						x	x	x	x	x		
Fingers: short						x	x	twisted	x	x		
Eyes: strong like light of sun				cat-like (gall color)			x		shining etc.	in eyes light etc.		
Right Eye: mixed with blood	x	x	x	x	x	x					x	x

Left Eye: glad	or: light blue					x	
green		x	?			?	
two pupils	x	x		x	x		
Eyes: other							*
Eyebrows: white	eyelids	x	x	eye-lashes	eye-lashes		
Lower Lip:	x	x	larger	larger	x		
Right Thigh: thin	x	x	x	x			
Right Foot: thin			and shins thin				
Feet: broad	x	x	x	x			

*   left: in it a spot   right: in it a sign

* right: very blue and in its pupil written: This is the false messiah

These texts bear only slight resemblances of substance to the
formally analogous passages of the Coptic Apocalypse of Elijah:
"aux jambes grêles; sur le devant de sa tête, il y a une touffe de
cheveux blancs; il est chauve; ses sourcils vont jusqu'aux oreilles;
sur le devant de ses mains il y a une tache de lèpre" [so most recently J.-M. Rosenstiehl, L'Apocalypse d'Elie (Textes et Etudes
pour ... le judaisme intertestamentaire 1; Paris: Geuthner, 1972)
98] and of the Hebrew Apocalypse of Elijah (M. Buttenweiser, p. 16):
"These will be his signs on which Daniel gazed: his face will be
long; a bald spot will be between his eyes; his stature will be
very tall; the soles of his feet will be high (? broad) and his
legs will be thin."

The same literary topos, physiognomic portraits of the Antichrist, is found in numerous other examples, which have, however,
no points of literary dependency on the above 12 texts. Most of
this material, with references to the discussion thereon, is con-
veniently assembled in J. M. Rosenstiehl's "Le Portrait de l'Antichrist," found in M. Philonenko, Pseudépigraphes de l'Ancien Testament et manuscrits de la Mer Morte (Paris: Presses Universitaires de
France, 1967) 45-60. The Coptic Apocalypse of Zephaniah quoted by
M.R. James, Apocrypha Anecdota I p. 155 is in fact the Coptic Apocalypse of Elijah to be printed in the second volume of the present
work; James refers also to Ps. Athanasius, Quaestiones ad Antiochum
Ducem 108 (Migne, PG. 28.664) cf. ibid. 109. These formal parallels
come from non-Elianic apocrypha, e.g. the Apocryphal Apocalypse of
Esdras (cf. C. Tischendorf, Apocalypses Apocryphae [Leipzig: 1866;
rep. Hildesheim: Olms, 1966] 28-29), the two forms of the apocryphal Apocalypse of John (cf. C. Tischendorf, ibid. 74-75), the
Falasha Book of Baruch (cf. J. Halévy, op. cit., 58, 179), the
Armenian Seventh Vision of Daniel (cf. G. Kalemkiar, "Die siebente
Vision Daniels," WZKM 6 [1892] 133, 239 and J. Issaverdens, Uncan-
onical Writings of the Old Testament[2] [Venice: Mechitarist Press,
1934] 263), the Persian Daniel-Nâmeh (cf. A. Wünsch, Aus Israels
Lehrhallen, II 71), some Latin miscellanea (Corpus Christi 404
fol. 7, Montpellier H. 405 fol. III, both texts translated by
Rosenstiehl, op. cit. 47-8), the Hebrew Book of Zerubbabel

(= Jellinek, Bet ha-Midrasch 2.27), the Hebrew Prayer of Shimeon
ben Yoḥai (Jellinek, ibid. 4.124), The Signs of the Messiah (Jellinek, ibid. 2.60), two portraits in the Hebrew Mysteries of Shimeon
ben Yoḥai (Jellinek, ibid. 3.79, 80), and Midrash Wayoshaʳ (Jellinek,
ibid. 1.55). Cf. also Rosenstiehl, op. cit. 47 on el-Bokhari, and
Ibn el-Wardi's Haridat el Ajâ'ib, translated by R. Basset, Les
Apocryphes Ethiopiens 10.79, 82. Rosenstiehl (op. cit. 53-4)
discusses the possibility of relating to the tradition of portraits
of the Antichrist the description of Caligula in Seneca, de Cons-
tantia 18 and Suetonius,Caligula 50.

We may also compare other physiognomic texts where, however, no
portrait of the Antichrist survives, both from Qumrân (cf. 4Q 186
[DJD V, 88-91], J. Starcky, "Un Texte messianique de Qumrân,"Ecole de
Langues orientales anciennes de l'Institut Catholique de Paris;
Mémorial du Cinquantennaire 1914-1964 [Travaux de l'Institut
Catholique de Paris 10; Paris: Bloud & Gay, 1964] 51-66, and A.
Dupont Sommer [CRAIBL, 1965, 239-253]) and in Greek (cf. R. Foerster,
Scriptores physiognomici Graeci et Latini [Leipzig: Teubner, 1893]).
Jewish physiognomic texts of ancient date were published by G.
Scholem, "Ein Fragment zur Physiognomik und Chiromantik aus der
spätantiken jüdischen Esoterik," Liber Amicorum - Studies in Honour
of Prof. Dr. C.J. Bleeker (Leiden: Brill, 1969) 174-194. Further
Hebrew fragments were published by I. Gruenwald, "Further Jewish
Physiognomic and Chiromantic Fragments," Tarbiẓ 40 (1971) 301-319
[in Hebrew].

Fragment III

"EYE HATH NOT SEEN"

42

Fragment III "Eye hath not seen".

The citation found in 1 Cor 2:9-10, attributed to the Apocryphon
or Apocalypse of Elijah by ancient authorities, occurs in many
other possibly independent forms. Another sentence perhaps quoted
from the same writing occurs in connection with it in Clem. Alex.,
Protrepticus 10.94.4 (IIIg below).

>IIIa. But, as it is written, "the things which eye did not see
>and ear did not hear, and which did not come up into a man's
>heart, which God prepared for those that love Him" God has re-
>vealed to us through the Spirit.
>
>[1 Cor 2:9-10]

>IIIb. 7. Therefore, we too must gather together with concord
>in our conscience and cry earnestly to him, as it were with one
>mouth, that we may share in his great and glorious promises.
>8. For he says, "Eye did not see, and ear did not hear, nor
>did it come up into a man's heart, how much He prepared for
>those that wait upon Him."
>[Clem. Rom. 1,34,8; tr. Kirsopp Lake, Apostolic Fathers (LCL;
> London & Cambridge: 1912) I.67.]

>IIIc. If then we perform righteousness before God, we will
>enter into His kingdom, and receive the promises which ear did
>not hear and eye did not see, nor did it come up into a man's
>heart.
>[Clem. Rom. 2,11,7; cf. 2,14,5: declare "what the Lord has
> prepared for His elect".]

9 ἀλλὰ καθὼς γέγραπται· "ἃ ὀφθαλμὸς οὐκ εἶδεν καὶ οὖς οὐκ
ἤκουσεν καὶ ἐπὶ καρδίαν ἀνθρώπου οὐκ ἀνέβη, ἃ ἡτοίμασεν ὁ
θεὸς τοῖς ἀγαπῶσιν αὐτόν." 10 ἡμῖν δὲ ἀπεκάλυψεν ὁ θεὸς
διὰ τοῦ πνεύματος.

9 εἶδεν] οἶδεν | ἃ] ὅσα   10 ὁ θεός ἀπεκάλυψεν |
δὲ] γάρ

H. von Soden, Die Schriften des Neuen Testaments, II (Gottingen:
Vandenhoeck and Ruprecht, 1913) 695.

7 καὶ ἡμεῖς οὖν ἐν ὁμονοίᾳ ἐπὶ τὸ αὐτὸ συναχθέντες τῇ
συνειδήσει, ὡς ἐξ ἑνὸς στόματος βοήσωμεν πρὸς αὐτὸν ἐκτενῶς
εἰς τὸ μετόχους ἡμᾶς γενέσθαι τῶν μεγάλων καὶ ἐνδόξων
ἐπαγγελιῶν αὐτοῦ. 8 λέγει γάρ· Ὀφθαλμὸς οὐκ εἶδεν καὶ οὖς
οὐκ ἤκουσεν καὶ ἐπὶ καρδίαν ἀνθρώπου οὐκ ἀνέβη ὅσα ἡτοίμασεν
τοῖς ὑπομένουσιν αὐτόν.
ὀφθαλμὸς A] ἃ ὀφθ. HLS Clem Al (I Cor. 2:9) | ὅσα AH] ἃ
L Clem Al,>S | ἡτοίμασεν A] + κύριος HLS | ὑπομένουσιν
AL] ἀγαπῶσιν HS

Funk-Bihlmeyer-Schneemelcher, Die Apostolische Väter, I (Tübingen:
J.C.B. Mohr, 1956) 53-54.

7 ἐὰν οὖν ποιήσωμεν τὴν δικαιοσύνην ἐναντίον τοῦ θεοῦ,
εἰσήξομεν εἰς τὴν βασιλείαν αὐτοῦ καὶ ληψόμεθα τὰς ἐπαγγελίας,
ἃς οὖς οὐκ ἤκουσεν οὐδὲ ὀφθαλμὸς εἶδεν, οὐδὲ ἐπὶ καρδίαν
ἀνθρώπου ἀνέβη.

Ibid, I, 76, 78.

44

IIId. And the fire of the inhuman torturers was cold to them;
for they held before their eyes the thought of flight from
that fire which is everlasting and never quenched, and with
the eyes of the heart they looked into those good things which
are kept for those that wait, which ear did not hear, and eye
did not see, and which did not come up into a man's heart, but
which were   shown unto them by the Lord, because they were
no longer men, but already angels.

[Mart. Polyc. 2.3]

IIIe. Who said to me, "This is enough for you, Isaiah; for
you have seen what no other son of flesh has seen, what neither eye has seen nor ear heard, nor has it come up into a
man's heart, how much God has prepared for all that love Him."
[Latin Ascensio Jesaiae 11.34. Insignificant variant in Slavonic. Ethiopic lacks the quotation.]

IIIf. Then the evil "shall depart into eternal punishment, but
the righteous shall go into eternal life (Matt 25:46)", inher-
iting those things which eye did not see and ear did not hear,
nor went up   into a man's heart, which God prepared for
those that love Him: and they shall rejoice in the kingdom of
God which is in Christ Jesus.

καὶ τὸ πῦρ ἦν αὐτοῖς ψυχρὸν τὸ τῶν ἀπανθρώπων βασανιστῶν·

πρὸ ὀφθαλμῶν γὰρ εἶχον φυγεῖν τὸ αἰώνιον καὶ μηδέποτε

σβεννύμενον, καὶ τοῖς τῆς καρδίας ὀφθαλμοῖς ἐνέβλεπον τὰ

τηρούμενα τοῖς ὑπομείνασιν ἀγαθά, ἃ οὔτε οὖς ἤκουσεν οὔτε

ὀφθαλμὸς εἶδεν οὔτε ἐπὶ καρδίαν ἀνθρώπου ἀνέβη, ἐκείνοις

δὲ ὑπεδείκνυτο ὑπὸ τοῦ κυρίου, οἵπερ μηκέτι ἄνθρωποι, ἀλλ'

ἤδη ἄγγελοι ἦσαν.

ἀπανθρώπων (ἀπανῶν) m Zahn Lightf.] ἀπηνῶν (ἀπεινῶν hp) g
Funk Hilgenf. | σβεννύμενον bhp] + πῦρ cmv Zahn
Hilgenf. | ἐνέβλεπον m Schw.] ἀνέβλεπον g Funk and ear-
lier eds. | εἶδεν cm] ἴδεν bhpv | δὲ + καὶ cv |
2 οἵπερ b] εἵπερ chpv, οἵτινες m | μηκέτι bchv] μὴ p,
λοιπὸν οὐκέτι m

Ibid, I, 121-122.

34 Qui dixit mihi: Sufficit tibi Ysaia; vidisti ⌐enim,⌐ quod
nemo ⌐alius⌐ vidit carnis filius, quod nec oculus vidit,
nec auris audivit, nec in cor hominis ascendit, quanta praeparavit deus omnibus diligentibus se[1].

1 S eum

R.H. Charles, The Ascension of Isaiah (London: A. and C. Black,
1900) 137

5 Τότε ἀπελεύσονται οἱ μὲν πονηροὶ εἰς αἰώνιον κόλασιν, οἱ
δὲ δίκαιοι πορεύσονται εἰς ζωὴν αἰώνιον, κληρονομοῦντες
ἐκεῖνα, ἃ ὀφθαλμὸς οὐκ εἶδεν καὶ οὖς οὐκ ἤκουσεν καὶ ἐπὶ
καρδίαν ἀνθρώπου οὐκ ἀνέβη, ἃ ἡτοίμασεν ὁ θεὸς τοῖς ἀγαπῶσιν
αὐτόν· καὶ χαρήσονται ἐν τῇ βασιλείᾳ τοῦ θεοῦ τῇ ἐν Χριστῷ
Ἰησοῦ.

46

[Apostolic Constitutions 7.32.5]

IIIg. Whence Scripture properly proclaims to those who have believed "But the Saints of the Lord will inherit the glory of God and His power." Tell me, o blessed one, what sort of glory? "Which eye did not see and ear did not hear, nor did it come up into a man's heart. And they will rejoice in the kingdom of their Lord for ever, Amen"

[Clem. Alex,Protrepticus 10.94.4: Stählin also attributes the first quotation in this passage to the Apocalypse of Elijah]

IIIh. As for the righteous, who will have walked in the way of righteousness, they will inherit the Lord's glory and His power. And to them will be given his strength, which no eye has seen nor ear heard. And they shall rejoice in My Kingdom.

[Testament of Our Lord and Redeemer Jesus Christ in Galilee (ed. Guerrier & Grebaut) 187]

IIIi. And then will I take them (i.e. the stones that are to be put by Cenez into the Ark of the Covenant) and many others far better than them, from that (place?   ) which eye has not seen nor ear heard and which has not come up into man's heart, until something like this come to pass in the world. And the righteous shall have no need of the light of the sun or of the brightness of the moon, for the light of these pre-

F.X. Funk, Doctrina Duodecim Apostolorum etc. (Tübingen: Laup, 1887) 96

ὅθεν ἡ γραφὴ εἰκότως εὐαγγελίζεται τοῖς πεπιστευκόσιν· "οἱ δὲ ἅγιοι κυρίου κληρονομήσουσι τὴν δόξαν τοῦ θεοῦ καὶ τὴν δύναμιν αὐτοῦ." ποίαν, ὦ μακάριε, δόξαν, εἰπέ μοι· "ἣν ὀφθαλμὸς οὐκ εἶδεν οὐδὲ οὖς ἤκουσεν, οὐδὲ ἐπὶ καρδίαν ἀνθρώπου ἀνέβη· καὶ χαρήσονται ἐπὶ τῇ βασιλείᾳ τοῦ κυρίου αὐτῶν εἰς τοὺς αἰῶνας, ἀμήν."

O. Stählin, Clemens Alexandrinus I, 3ed. rev. U. Treu,(GCS 12; Berlin: Akademie Verlag, 1972) 69, lines 14-19 = P.G. VIII, 208B-C

Schmidt and Wajnberg, op. cit. (Fg. IIe) 66*; Guerrier and Grébaut, op. cit. (Fg. IIe) 187

115   · · · ·/ habitantes terram.   Et
tunc accipiam et istos et alios plures valde meliores, ex
eo quod oculus non vidit nec auris audivit, et in cor hominis
non ascendit, quousque tale aliquid fieret in seculum.   Et
non indigent iusti opera luminis solis neque splendore
lune, quoniam preciosissimorum lapidum lumen erit lumen
eorum.

cious stones will be their light.

[Pseudo-Philo, Biblical Antiquities XXVI.13]

IIIj. The Epistula Titi, which knew the Elijah apocalypse (cf. fg
1a supra) also quotes this passage, perhaps directly from Elijah,
attributing to the Lord the saying

> Great and noble is the divine promise which the Lord by His
> own mouth promised to His saints and pure ones, that He would
> give them what eyes had not seen nor ears heard, nor had it
> come up into man's heart, and that they would be for ever and
> ever an incomparable and invisible race.

IIIk. And he said to me, "Just as you cannot do or say any one
of them, thus you will not be able to investigate the wisdom
of the Most High nor to know the power (MS H: variety) of his
paths, or to find His judgement, or the end of his love or the
good things from him which He has promised (MS H: + to give)
to his loved ones, which eye has not seen and ear has not
heard, nor has it fallen into the heart of (or: occurred to)
man, and which man has never thought of, which God prepared fo
His beloved ones."

[IV Ezra Armen. 5:40. Marginal note, secunda manu, in Erevan
MS 1500 (H) attributes Paul's quotation to Ezra (i.e. this re
cension of IV Ezra).]

117-118 fieret tale aliquid ∿ π | 118 seculo π recte? |
indigebunt P | opera luminis] lumine π | solis — lune om.
BCO | 119 lumen preciosissimorum lapidum ∿ π

Pseudo-Philon, Les Antiquités Bibliques (Sources Chrétiennes no.
229; introduction and text D.J. Harrington, tr. J. Cazeaux;
Paris: Editions du Cerf, 1976)1.210, 212. Cf. G. Kisch, Pseudo-
Philo's Liber Antiquitatum Biblicarum (Publications in Mediaeval
Studies 10; Notre Dame: U. of Notre Dame, 1949) 188.

Magna est atque honesta pollicitacio diuina quam ore suo
dominus promisit sanctis ac inmaculatis daturum se eis quod
non uiderunt oculi[s], nec aures audierunt, nec in cor hominis
ascendit, et erit in aeternis aeternorum gens inconparabilis
et inconspicibilis.

de Bruyne, op. cit. (Fg. Ia) 48

Եւ ասէ ցիս՝ որպէս ոչ կարես ի նոցանէս մի ինչ առնել կամ
ասել, նոյնպէս ոչ կարասցես զիմաստութիւն.Բարձրելոյն
քննել եւ զիտել զգօրութիւն[1] ճանապարհաց նորա եւ կամ
զտանել զդատաստանս նորա կամ զվախճան սիրոյ նորա՝ զոր
խոստացաւ[2] սիրելեաց իւրոց եւ կամ առ ի նմանէ զբարիսն,
զոր ակն ոչ ետես եւ ունկն ոչ լուաւ եւ սիրտ մարդոյ ոչ
անկալ եւ ոչ զմտաւ երբէք ած մարդ՝ զոր պատրաստեաց
Աստուած սիրելեաց իւրոց:

   1 զրնդրութիւն H   2 + տալ H
M.E. Stone, Concordance and Texts of Armenian IV Ezra (Oriental
Notes and Studies II; Jerusalem: Israel Oriental Society, 1971)
16-18.

IIIl. Partial quotations, i.e. of only the first part of this text, may be derived from 1 Cor 2:9 or even from its source in Isa 64:43 (combined with Isa 65:16, Jer 3:16, Sir 1:10); in any case it has had wide distribution in Judaism, Christianity and even Islam. Furthermore, as a natural literary topos, similar expressions occur passim in classical and modern literature.

IIIm. A dominical saying:

a) "Jesus said. I will give you what eye has not seen and what ear has not heard and what hand has not touched and (what) has not come up into the heart of man."
[Gospel of Thomas, Logion 17]

b) "You also then, brethren, having taken refuge in Him and learnt that in Him alone you exist, will attain those things of which He says to us 'what neither eye saw nor ear heard nor did they come up into the heart of man.' We pray to Thee then for those things Thou has promised to give, immaculate Jesus. We praise Thee,..."
[Martyrium Petri, 10]

c) "You also then, having taken refuge in Him and hoping all things in Him, may this happen to you that the things you have learnt may be able to abide in you, so that you may be able to attain unto those things which He has promised to give, "things which neither eye has seen nor ear heard nor has it come up into the heart of sinful man" praying Him for those things which He promised to give. We pray Thee, Lord Jesus, and..."

ⲡⲉϪⲉ ⲓ̅ⲥ̅ Ϫⲉ ϯⲛⲁϯ ⲚⲎⲦⲚ̅ Ⲙ̅ⲠⲈⲦⲈ Ⲙ̅ⲠⲈⲂⲀⲖ ⲚⲀⲨ ⲈⲢⲞϤ
ⲀⲨⲰ ⲠⲈⲦⲈ Ⲙ̅ⲠⲈⲘⲀ ⲀϪⲈ ⲤⲞⲦⲘⲈϤ· ⲀⲨⲰ ⲠⲈⲦⲈ Ⲙ̅ⲠⲈⲤⲓϪ ⲤⲘ̅-
ⲤⲰⲘϤ̅· ⲀⲨⲰ Ⲙ̅ⲠⲈϤⲈⲒ ⲈϨⲢⲀⲒ̈ ϨⲒ ϤⲎⲦ` Ⲣ̅ⲢⲰⲘⲈ

A. Guillaumont et alii (edd.), The Gospel according to Thomas
(Leiden: Brill, 1959) 12

6 ἐπὶ τοῦτον ⁶/ οὖν καὶ ὑμεῖς, ἀδελφοί, καταφυγόντες καὶ ἐν αὐτῷ μόνῳ
τὸ / ὑπάρχειν ὑμᾶς μαθόντες, ἐκείνων τεύξεσθε, ὧν λέγει ὑμῖν· ἃ /
οὔτε ὀφθαλμὸς εἶδεν, οὔτε οὖς ἤκουσεν, οὔτε   ἐπὶ καρδίαν /
10ἀνθρώπου οὐκ ἀνέβη. αἰτοῦμεν οὖν περὶ ὧν ἡμῖν ὑπέσχου / δοῦναι,
ἀμίαντε Ἰησοῦ· αἰνοῦμέν σε,...

    6 ημησ (ἡμεῖς) P | καταφυγ. προσεύξασθε S   7 ημασ P | τεύξασθε
    P | ἐκείνου τεύξεσθε ἀγαπητοὶ ὃν λέγει δοῦναι ὑμῖν ὑπῖσχούμενος A
    8 ἴδεν AP | οὔτε οὖς ἤκουσεν om P sed extat in ACS   9 ἀνθρ.
    ἁμαρτωλοῦ S consentiente V | οὐκ om A | αἰτοῦμεν] δεόμενοιA
    10 ἀμίαντε Ἰησ. αἰν. σε om. A.

R. Lipsius (ed.), Acta Apostolorum Apocrypha I (repr.; Darmstadt:
Wissensch. Buchgesellschaft, 1959) 98.

    in hunc autem | et uos refugientes et in eum omnia |

    sperantes, hoc constet in uos | ut quae didicistis possint

    per/ma|nere in uobis, ut possitis ad ea per||uenire quae

    promisit se datu<rum>, | quae neque oculus uidit, nequ<e

10 auris> | audiuit,   neque in cor hominis pecca<toris> |

    ascendit, praecantes eum de qui<bus> | promisit se

    datu<rum>. oramus te d<omine> | Iesu et

52

[Actus Petri cum Simone, 39]

IIIn. Rabbinic usages show similar conflates of Isa 64:3; cf. H.L.
Strack and P. Billerbeck, Kommentar z. N.T., 3.327-9.

a) Rabbi Levi said: Come and see how great is the good that
the Holy One Blessed be He has laid up for the righteous for
the future which is to come, as it says, (Ps 31:20 (19))
"O how abundant is Thy goodness which Thou hast laid up for
those who fear Thee, and wrought for those who take refuge
in Thee in the sight of the sons of men!" The text here does
not say "among themselves" rather it says "in the sight of
the sons of men", that is, in the sight of all the sons of
the world. R. Yoḥanan says: It should not be interpreted
thus, but rather that there is shown to the eye what it is
capable of seeing and there is made heard to the ear what it
is capable of hearing, but that which He has ordained for the
righteous for the future which is to come the eye cannot see
nor can the ear hear, as it says (Isa 64:3) "no eye has seen
a God beside Thee, who works for him who waits for Him."
[Midrash Mishlé 13:25, 37a]

b) 'Let it suffice you' (lit: it is much for you) (Deut 3:26).
He said to him, "Much is kept for you, and much is laid up
for you, as it says (Ps 31:20 (19))"O how abundant is Thy
goodness which Thou hast laid up for those who fear Thee."
And it says (Isa 64:3) "For of old no one has heard or perceived by the ear, no eye has seen a God besides Thee, who
works for him who waits for Him."
[Sifré Num 27:12]

Lipsius (ed.), ibid., 99.

אמר ר' לוי בא וראה כמה גדול הטוב שצפן הקב"ה לצדיקים לעתיד לבא,
שנמאר מה רב טובך אשר צפנת ליראיך פעלת לחוסים בך נגד בני אדם
(תהילים לא.כ), בינם לבינם אינו אומר כאן, אלא נגד בני אדם, נגד
כל בני העולם.   ר' יוחנן אומר לא כן אלא מראין לעין מה שיכולה
לראות, ומשמיעין לאוזן מה שיכולה לשמוע, אבל מה שהתקין לצדיקים
לעתיד לבוא, לא עין יכולה לראות, ולא אוזן יכולה לשמוע, שנאמר
עין לא ראתה אלהים זולתך יעשה למחכה לו (ישעי' סד.ג).

S. Buber (ed.), Midrash Mishle (Wilna: Rom, 1892) 37a.

רב לך אמר לו הרבה שמור לך הרבה צפון לך שנאמר מה רב טובך אשר
צפנת ליראיך (תילים לא) ואומר ומעולם לא שמעו ולא האזינו עין
לא ראתה אלהים זולתך יעשה למחכה לו(ישעיה סד).

H.S. Horovitz (ed.), Siphre d'be Rab (Jerusalem: Wahrmann, 1966) 181.

c) A somewhat different attestation is to be found in an early
mystical work, the Re'uyoth Yehezkel. Following a lacuna, the
text reads:

> For thus the Holy One Blessed be He said to Ezekiel: 'On con-
> dition I show you My Chariot, so that you may explain (it)
> to Israel. As it says (Ezek 40:3), "Declare all that you
> see to the house of Israel." And it says: (Ezek 3:10-11),
> "Moreover He said to me, 'Son of man, all My words that I
> shall speak to you receive in your heart and hear with your
> ears. And go, get you to the exiles, to your people, etc.",
> but rather to teach man those things which the eye can see
> and which the ear can hear.'"

[Re'uyoth Yehezkel, ed. Gruenwald, pp. 100-101, and note there]

IIIo. Gnostic uses (cf. T8a infra.)

a) Not only will I (the Soter) reveal to you all things after which you ask, but from now on I will also reveal to you
other (things) which you have not thought to ask after, which
have not come up into the heart of man, and which also all
the Gods who are beneath men do not know.
[Pistis Sophia ch. 114 (Schwartze-Petermann 297)]

b) Manichean. "in order that I may redeem you from death
and destruction, I will give you what you have not seen with
the eye nor heard with the ear nor grasped with the hand."
[Turfan Frags. M 554, M 789]

שכך אמר לו הקב״ה ליחזקאל, על תניי אני מראה אותך את המרכבה שלי כדי שתפריש להם לישראל,שנ׳: ״הגד את כל אשר אתה רואה לבית ישי״ (יחז׳ מ.4) ואו׳ : ״ויאמר אלי בן אדם את כל אשר אדבר אליך קח בלבבך ובאזניך שמע ולך בא אל הגולה אל בני עמך וגו׳״. (יחז׳ ג׳ 11-10), אלא לדורשן לאדם מה שהעין יכולה לראות ומה שהאוזן יכולה לשמוע.

1. Gruenwald, "Re'uyoth Yeḥezkel," Temirin 1 (1972) 100-101.

ⲛⲏⲧⲛ̄ ϫⲉ ⲟⲩⲙⲟⲛⲟⲛ ϯⲛⲁϭⲱⲗⲡ̄ ⲛⲏⲧⲛ̄ ⲉⲃⲟⲗ ⲛ̄ϩⲱⲃ ⲛⲓⲙ ⲉⲧⲉⲧⲛⲁϣⲓⲛⲉ ⲛ̄ⲥⲱⲟⲩ· ⲁⲗⲗⲁ ϫⲓⲛ ⲧⲉⲛⲟⲩ ⲟⲛ ϯⲛⲁϭⲱⲗⲡ̄ ⲛⲏⲧⲛ̄ ⲉⲃⲟⲗ ⲛ̄ϩⲉⲛⲕⲟⲟⲩⲉ ⲛⲁⲓ̈ ⲉⲧⲉ ⲙ̄ⲡⲉⲧⲛ̄ⲛⲟⲓ̈ ⲙ̄ⲙⲟⲟⲩ ⲉϣⲓⲛⲉ ⲛ̄ⲥⲱⲟⲩ· ⲛⲁⲓ̈ ⲉⲧⲉ ⲙ̄ⲡⲟⲩⲁⲗⲉ ⲉϫⲙ̄ ⲡϩⲏⲧ ⲛ̄ⲣⲣⲱⲙⲉ· ⲛⲁⲓ̈ ⲉⲧⲉ ⲛ̄ⲥⲉⲥⲟⲟⲩⲛ ⲙ̄ⲙⲟⲟⲩ ⲁⲛ ⲛϭⲓ ⲛ̄ⲕⲉⲛⲟⲩⲧⲉ ⲧⲏⲣⲟⲩ ⲉⲧϩⲛ̄ ⲛ̄ⲣⲱⲙⲉ·

C. Schmidt, Pistis Sophia (Coptica 2; Hauniae: Gylderdalske Boghandel-Nordisk Forlag, 1925) 296.

//////

bôžâ////

'abnâ////[s]

'asmâh kê čašm

padên nê dîd gôšân nê

'ašnûd 'ûṭ nê grîft

56

c) Manichean. In this way everything which has happened
and which will happen was revealed to me through the Paraclete: "What the eye sees and the ear hears and thought thinks
and [   ] through him (i.e. the Paraclete) I have
seen everything and I became 'one body and one spirit'."
[Kephalaia 15, 19ff.]

d) Nag Hammadi. The Lord said, "[You (sing.) have] asked
me for a word [about that] which eye has not seen, nor have
I heard about it,...."
[Dialogue of the Saviour, CG III, 5 (140.1-4)]

pad dast////ḥ////îy̠ 'abar

//////

////m nêdfûrd////

////qûtân bôžân

'aǰ maran 'ûd 'abnâs dahân

'ô 'îšmâh kê čašm padên

nê dîd gôšân nê 'išnûd ûd nê

grîft pad dast hô kê abar bazakarâ[n]

F.W.K. Müller, "Handschriften-Reste in Estrangelo-Schrift aus
Turfan, 2," Pr. Ak. Wiss. Berlin, Phil.-Hist. Kl. Abh. (1904)
Abhang II, 67-68

ⲦⲌⲈ ⲦⲈ ⲦⲈⲒ̈ ⲈⲦⲀ ⲌⲰ ⲚⲒⲘ Ⲉ[Ⲧ]Ⲁ[Ⲱ]
ⲠⲈ ⲘⲚ ⲠⲈ ⲚⲀⲰⲠⲈ ⲤⲰⲀⲠ ⲚⲎⲒ ⲀⲂⲀⲖ ⲌⲘ
ⲠⲠⲢⲔⲖⲤ ⲘⲠ .. Ⲛ ..
ⲌⲰ ⲚⲒⲘ Ⲉ̧ⲀⲢⲈ ⲠⲂⲈⲖ Ⲓ̈ⲀⲢⲌ ⲚⲦⲈ ⲠⲘ̧ⲦⲈ
ⲤⲀⲦⲘⲈ ⲚⲦⲈ ⲠⲘⲀ
ⲔⲘⲈⲔ ⲘⲈⲔⲘⲞⲨⲔ Ⲛ[Ⲧ]Ⲉ ⲠⲈ.Ⲁ ⲀⲦ...
Ⲁ̈ⲘⲘⲈ Ⲛ̄ⲌⲎⲦ Ⲁ̧
ⲌⲰ ⲚⲒⲘ Ⲁ̈ⲒⲚⲈⲨ ⲀⲠⲦⲎⲢ ⲚⲦⲞⲞⲦ Ⲁ̈Ⲣ ⲞⲨⲤⲰⲘⲀ
ⲚⲞⲨⲰⲦ
ⲘⲚ ⲞⲠ̄Ⲛ̄Ⲁ ⲚⲞⲨⲰⲦ

"Kephalaia," mit einem Beitrag von H. Ibscher: Manichäische Hss.
der staatlichen Museen Berlin, ed. C. Schmidt (Stuttgart: Kohlhammer,
1940) 15.19-24.

ⲠⲈⲆⲈ ⲠⲆⲞⲉ̧[ⲒⲤ ⲆⲈ ⲀⲔ]ⲰⲒⲚⲈ Ⲙ̄ⲘⲞⲈⲒ
ⲈⲨⲰⲈⲆⲈ̧ [ⲈⲦⲂⲈ ⲠⲀ]Ⲓ ⲈⲦⲈ Ⲙ̄ⲠⲈⲂⲀⲖ
ⲚⲀⲨ ⲈⲢⲞ [Ⲟ]Ⲩ̧Ⲁ̧Ⲉ̧ Ⲙ̄ⲠⲒⲤⲞⲦⲘⲈ

Translation by H. Attridge apud J.M. Robinson (ed.), The Nag Hammadi
Library in English (San Francisco: Harper and Row, 1977) 236.

e) Nag Hammadi. Grant what no angel-eye has [seen] and no archon-ear <has> heard and what [has not] entered into the human heart...

[Prayer of the Apostle Paul, CG I.1 (A.23-27)]

IIIp. Islamic

Abu Hureira reports that the Messenger of God said "God has said these words 'I have prepared for my servants, the right-eous, things which no eye has seen, which no ear has heard, which have never come into the mind of any human being'."

[Al Buḥari, on Sura 32]

IIIq.   And let these words of Empedocles be constantly in mind "Nor are these things to be seen of man, nor to be heard, nor with the mind to be comprehended."

[Empedocles apud Plutarchum, De Poetis Audiendis. 17E]

IIIr. From a dialogue on the soul, perhaps originally Greek but surviving only in Syriac; attributed to Socrates conversing with one Herostrophus.

But I say to you, O Herostrophus, that these three things will bring them to a pleasant place of rest which eyes do not see, nor ears hear of it, not does the mouth speak of it; but by these three things incorporeally purely one comes to that place which is the primeval origin. Because it is impossible, O Herostrophus, for these things to exist in space except where there is for them a place where they may be preserved in uprightness purely and chastely. But if there are men in whom these three things exist, ...

ⲉⲣⲓ ⲭⲁⲣⲓⲍⲉ ⲛ[ϩⲉⲓ] ⲙ̄ⲡⲉⲧⲉⲛⲡⲉ̄ⲃⲉⲗ
ⲛⲁⲅⲅⲉⲗⲟⲥ [ⲛⲉⲩ] ⲁⲣⲁⲩ ⲁⲩⲱ ⲡⲉⲧⲉⲙⲙ̄-
ⲉⲯⲭⲉ [ⲛⲁ]ⲣⲭⲱⲛ ⲥⲁⲧⲙⲉⲩ ⲁⲩⲱ ⲡⲉⲧⲉ
[ⲙⲡⲉ]ⲩⲉⲓ̂ ⲁ̄ⲣⲏⲓ ⲅⲙ ⲫⲏⲧ' ⲛ̄ⲣⲱⲙⲉ

R. Kasser, et al., Oratio Pauli Apostoli in Tractatus Tripartitus
II and III (Bern: Franke, 1975) 248. Translation by D. Müller
from ibid., 28.

For references to numerous sources see:

A.J. Wensinck, Concordance et Indices de la tradition musulmane
(Leiden: 1955) 3.337.

καὶ τὰ Ἐμπεδοκλέους ἔστω πρόχειρα ταυτί· /οὕτως οὔτ'
ἐπιδερκτὰ τάδ' ἀνδράσιν οὔτ' ἐπακουστὰ /οὔτε νόῳ περιληπτά,

Plutarch, Moralia, I ed. F.C. Babbitt(Loeb Cl. Lib.; London and
Cambridge Mass.; Heinemann and Harvard, 1960) 90.

[Syriac text, 6 lines]

[Anonymous; <u>Dialogue of Socrates with Herostrophus, On the</u>

<u>Soul</u>; cf. A. Baumstark, <u>Geschichte der syrischen Literatur</u>

(Bonn; Marcus and Weber, 1922) 169]

IIIs. From the Ethiopic version of Ps. Callisthenes' <u>Life of Alex-</u>
<u>ander the Great</u>:

<u>Hitherto eye hath not seen, and hitherto ear hath not heard,</u>
<u>neither can be described or conceived by the mind the things</u>
<u>which God hath prepared</u> for those who have endured patiently
from the creation of the world; but for the fiends and devils
and for the sinners He hath prepared punishment and the flame
of fire from which there is no escape for ever and for ever.
[Budge (tr.), <u>Alexander</u>,2.539]

IIIt. From the Falasha Ethiopic Ezra Apocalypse:

Ceux qui auront observé ce jour du sabbat ... jouiront du
repos ... qui sera pour eux la récompense et le partage <u>que</u>
<u>Dieu leur a préparés avant le monde, ce que l'oeil ne peut</u>
<u>voir, ce que l'oreille ne peut entendre et ce que la pensée</u>
<u>de l'homme ne peut imaginer: voilà ce que Dieu a destiné à</u>
<u>ses élus qui l'auront aimé</u>.
[Halévy (tr.) <u>Tĕ'ĕzâza Sanbat</u>, 180-181]

IIIu. Other variant forms found in patristic literature are probably to be considered free variations on 1 Cor 2:9 or on Isa 64:3:

a) For unto those who, with perseverance, through good works
seek incorruptibility, He will give everlasting life, joy,

P. Lagardii, <u>Analecta Syriaca</u> (Leipzig: B.G. Teubner, 1858) 161, ll. 10-18.

E.A.W. Budge, <u>The Life and Exploits of Alexander the Great</u> (London: Clay, 1896)1.340, ll. 16-20.

Halévy, <u>op</u>. <u>cit</u>. (Fg. IIk) 60.

τοῖς μὲν καθ᾽ ὑπομονὴν διὰ ἔργων ἀγαθῶν ζητοῦσιν τὴν

ἀφθαρσίαν δωρήσεται ζωὴν αἰώνιον, χαράν, εἰρήνην, ἀνάπαυσιν

62

peace, rest, and abundance of those good things which 'eye ...
heart of man' (1 Cor 2:9); but to the unfaithful ...
[Theophilus, Ad Autolycum, I 14,13]

b)   Just as in Isaiah 'Ye shall eat all good things of the
earth' will be understood of the good things of the flesh,
which await the flesh when it has been reshaped in the kingdom of God, made angelic, and when it will attain those things
which neither eye ... heart of man (1 Cor 2:9)
[Tertullian, De resurrectione mortuorum 26.7]

c)   But we speak concerning the upper world, concerning God
and angels, concerning Watchers and Holy ones, concerning
the food of immortality and the drink of the true vine, concerning garments that endure and grow not old, concerning
which 'eye...of sinful man which God has prepared for those
that love him' (1 Cor 2:9; cf. IIIj). Concerning these things
do we converse and . . . "
[Acts of Thomas 36]

καὶ πλήθη ἀγαθῶν, 13 ὧν οὔτε ὀφθαλμὸς εἶδεν οὔτε οὖς
ἤκουσεν οὔτε ἐπὶ καρδίαν ἀνθρώπου ἀνέβη· τοῖς δὲ ἀπίστοις

J.C.T. Otto (ed.), <u>Corpus Apologetarum Christianorum</u>, VIII (1861,
repr. Wiesbaden: 1969) 44.

Sicut[1] et apud Esaiam: Bona terrae edetis bona carnis
intellegentur,[2] quae illam manent in regno dei reformatam[3]
et angeli|ficatam et consecuturam quae nec oculus[4] uidit
nec auris audiuit nec in cor hominis ascenderunt.[5]

1 Sicut T: sic M P X   2 intelleguntur T   3 deformatam T
4 nec oculus] oculsn̄ T (sn̄ al. m. in ras.)   5 ascenderunt
T X R: ascendit M P (corr. R)

Tertullian, <u>Opera, Volumen II</u> ed. J.G.P. Borleffs (Corpus
Christianorum 2; Turnholti: Brepols, 1954) 954-5.

0 ἀλλὰ λέγομεν περὶ τὸν ἄνω κόσμον, 1 περὶ θεοῦ καὶ ἀγγέλων,
περὶ ἐγρηγόρων καὶ ἀγίων, περὶ τῆς 2 ἀμβροσιώδους τροφῆς καὶ
τοῦ ποτοῦ τῆς ἀμπέλου τῆς ἀληθι- 3 -νῆς, περὶ ἐνδυμάτων
παραμόνων καὶ μὴ παλαιουμένων, περὶ 4 ὧν ὀφθαλμὸς οὐκ εἶδεν
οὐδὲ οὖς ἤκουσεν, οὐδὲ ἐπὶ καρδίαν 5 ἀνθρώπων ἁμαρτωλῶν
ἀνέβη,   ἃ ὁ θεὸς ἡτοίμασεν τοῖς ἀγα- 6 -πῶσιν αὐτόν.   περὶ
τούτων διαλεγόμεθα καὶ

0 των ἄνω κοσμων U , του ἄνω κοσμου probabilius Thilo & Tisch.
1 π. ἐγ. κ. ἀγ. (f) om D. P | γρηγόρων U: ἐγρ. <πνευμάτων>?
Syr | 2 κ. τ. π. -ἀλ. om D | ἀμπ. τ. ἀλ.] aquae uitalis Syr
ueri uini albi   (om τ. ποτ.) Eth| 3 παρ. κ.] τῶν P |
παραμενόντων D: cf 152,1; 155,4; c 61e; 66e; 124 m | παλ]
καὶ ἀφθάρτων bis add P | 4 οὐδε prius] καὶ P | οὖς P
οὐκ add PY | οὐδε <u>alt</u>] καὶ P | 5 ἀμ.] οὐκ add PY |

IIIv. There are countless further parallels in world literature which could be cited; let one do duty for all. W. Shakespeare, Midsummer Night's Dream, Act IV, Sc 1 (end)

As to the derivation of any of these forms from an apocryphon of Elijah, the evidence is divided.

a) Attributions of 1 Cor 2:9 to Elijah

IIIa T1   This testimony (i.e. Matt 27:9) is found in the apocrypha of Jeremiah; just as the Apostle (Paul) quotes certain apocryphal writings, such as that passage "What the eye did not see, nor ear hear." For this is found in no canonical book, except in the apocrypha of Elijah the Prophet.
[Origen on Matt 27:9; 23, 37]

IIIa T2   But, as it is written "what eye has not seen, nor ear heard, nor has it come up into the heart of man, what God has prepared for those that love Him" (1 Cor 2:9). This is written in the Apocalypse of Elijah, among the apocrypha.
[Ambrosiaster on 1 Cor]

5-6 ἦτ. τ. ἀ. ἀ.] τ. ἀ. ἀ. παρεσκεύασεν P || 5 παρεσκεύασεν
U ||

R.A. Lipsius et M. Bonnet (edd.), Acta Apostolorum Apocrypha, II.2
(Leipzig: H. Mendelsohn, 1903) 153-154.

Bottom: ... The eye of man hath not heard, the ear of man

hath not seen; man's hand is not able to taste, his tongue

to conceive, nor his heart to report what my dream was ...

.... in secretis Hieremiae hoc prophetatur, sciens

quoniam et apostolus scripturas quasdam secretorum profert,

sicut dicit alicubi (9) : Quod oculus non vidit, nec auris

audivit; in nullo enim regulari libro hoc positum invenitur,

nisi in secretis Eliae prophetae.

E. Klostermann (ed.), Origenes, xi (GCS 38; Leipzig: Hinrichs,
1933) 250; also found in Zacharias Chrysopolitanus, In Unum et
Quatuor iv.166 (Maxima Bibliotheca Patrum 19; Lugduni: Anissonios,
1677) 937.

2,9. Sed sicut scriptum est: quod oculus non vidit nec auris

audivit nec in cor hominis ascendit, quae praeparavit deus

diligentibus eum. 1. hoc scriptum est in apocalypsi

20 Heliae in apocryphis.

19 his qui diligunt Π E L | eum] se P   19sq. in Esaia
profeta aliis verbis Π E T L G² P D   20 apocalypsin W G¹

IIIa T3   In the first Epistle to the Corinthians there are
17 quotations; two from Genesis, the eighth and the sixteenth
in order in the epistle; one from Exodus, the tenth in order;
two from Deuteronomy, the seventh and ninth in order; one from
Kings, the same also from Jeremiah the prophet, the second in
order; one from Ps 23, the eleventh in order; one from Ps 93,
the sixth in order; one from Job, the fifth in order; one from
Hosea the prophet, the seventeenth in order; three from Isaiah,
the first, fourth, and thirteenth in order; one from the Gospel
according to Matthew, the twelfth in order; one from an apocryphon of Elijah, the third in order; one sententia from
Menander, the fifteenth in order (i.e. 15:33); and one Laconic
proverb of Demades, the fourteenth in order (15:32) ...

[Euthalius Diaconus, Editio XIV S. Pauli Ap. Epistolarum.]

IIIa T3b   Clearly related to the above (for it too is followed by
reference to Menander and the Laconic Proverb) is the following
passage of Photius, Ad Amphilochium quaestiones, 151:

And the blessed Paul in the <...> letter to the Corinthians
makes mention of this passage from the apocryphal works said
to be by the prophet Elijah,"Those things which eye saw not, and
ear heard not, nor did they come up into man's heart, what God
prepared for those who love Him".

IIIa T4   From the Apocrypha of Elijah, cf. Georgius Syncellus at
IV d 2 infra.

IIIa T5   Marginal notes in an XIth century MS (mentioned by Mont-
faucon Diarium Italicum, p. 212) and in MSS 607 and 1523 of the

Ambrosiastri, Comm. in Epp. Paulinas, II ed. H.I. Vogels (CSEL 81
.2; Vienna: Hölder-Pichler-Tempsky, 1968) 26 = P.L. 14.194-195

Ἐν τῇ πρὸς Κορινθίους πρώτῃ ἐπιστολῇ ιζ'. Γενέσεως ΙΙ·
η', ις'. Ἐξόδου Ι· ι'. Δευτερονομίου ΙΙ· ζ', θ'. Βασιλειῶν
πρώτης καὶ Ἱερεμίου προφήτου ἡ αὐτὴ Ι· β'. Ψαλμοῦ κγ', Ι·
ια'. Ψαλμοῦ ᴌγ', Ι· ς'. Ἰὼβ Ι· ε'. Ὠσηὲ προφήτου ιζ'. Ι.
Ἡσαΐου προφήτου ΙΙΙ· α', δ', ιγ'. Ἐκ τοῦ κατὰ Ματθαῖον
Εὐαγγελίου Ι· ιβ'. Ἡλία ἀποκρύφου Ι· γ'. Μενάνδρου γνώμη
Ι· ιε'. Δημάδου λακωνικὴ παροιμία Ι· ιδ'.

Euthalius Diac., Editio XIV S. Pauli Epp. = P.G. 85.721.

Ὁ δὲ μακάριος Παῦλος ἐν τῇ πρὸς Κορινθίους Ἐπιστολῇ ἐκ
τῶν λεγομένων τοῦ προφήτου Ἡλίου ἀποκρύφων ταύτης μνημονεύει
τῆς φωνῆς· "Ἃ ὀφθαλμὸς οὐκ εἶδε, καὶ οὖς οὐκ ἤκουσε, καὶ
ἐπὶ καρδίαν ἀνθρώπου οὐκ ἀνέβη, ἃ ἡτοίμασεν ὁ θεὸς τοῖς
ἀγαπῶσιν αὐτόν."

Migne, P.G. 101, 813   1 leg. τῇ <πρωτῇ>

Royal Library in France, mentioned by Cotelerius (<u>Patres Apostolici</u>
I p. 347) -- cf. J.A. Fabricius, <u>Codex Pseudepigraphus Veteris</u>
<u>Testamenti</u>[2] (Hamburg: T.C. Felginer, 1722) I.1072 n.

IIIa T6-T7   Jerome derives 1 Cor 2:9 directly from the Hebrew text
of Is 64:3 (literally "Yea from of old they have not heard, they
have not given ear. Eye has not seen, O God, (anyone) apart from
Thee, who works for those that wait for him."); he concedes, however, that the passage occurs both in the <u>Ascension of Isaiah</u> (cf.
III 5a <u>supra</u>.) and the <u>Apocalypse of Elijah</u>.

> T6. "From everlasting they have not heard, nor with their
>
> eyes perceived. Eye has not seen, O God, without Thee, the
>
> things Thou hast prepared for those that wait for Thee ..."
>
> LXX: "From everlasting we have not heard, nor have our eyes
>
> perceived, God, apart from Thee, and Thy works which Thou wilt
>
> do for those that wait for mercy ..." The Apostle Paul, in
>
> the epistle which he writes to the Corinthians, as "a Hebrew
>
> of the Hebrews" (Phil 3:5) uses a paraphrase of this testimony
>
> taken from the genuine canonical books, not rendering it word
>
> for word -- a thing he utterly despises doing -- but express-
>
> ing the true meaning of the terms which he uses to strengthen
>
> his contention. And so they should fall silent, those ravings
>
> of the Apocryphal writings which under the pretended authority
>
> of this passage have been introduced into Christ's churches --
>
> writings about which it can truly be said that "The Devil
>
> dwells in ambushes with the wealthy in hidden places (or
>
> "apocrypha", i.e. <u>in apocryphis</u>, which Jerome has substituted
>
> for the Roman Psalter's <u>in occultis</u>) in order to slay the
>
> innocent," (Ps 10:8), and again that "He lies in ambush in a
>
> hidden place (or "an apocryphon", i.e. <u>in apocrypho</u>, which again

4.5. A saeculo non audierunt, neque auribus perceperunt.
Oculus non uidit, Deus, absque te quae praeparasti exspectantibus te. Occurristi laetanti et facienti iustitiam in uiis
5   tuis; recordabuntur tui. LXX: A saeculo non audiuimus, neque
oculi nostri uiderunt Deum absque te, et opera tua, quae
facies exspectantibus misericordiam. Occurrit enim facien-
tibus iustitiam, et uiarum tuarum recordabuntur. Paraphrasim
huius testimonii, quasi Hebraeus ex Hebraeis, assumit apos-
10 tolus Paulus de authenticis libris in epistola quam scribit
ad Corinthios, non uerbum ex uerbo reddens, quod facere om-
nino contemnit, sed sensuum exprimens ueritatem, quibus
utitur ad id quod uoluerit roborandum. Vnde apocryphorum
deliramenta conticeant, quae ex occasione huius testimonii
15 ingeruntur ecclesiis Christi. De quibus uere dici potest,
quod sedeat diabolus in insidiis cum diuitibus in apocryphis,
ut interficiat innocentem. Et iterum: Insidiatur in apocrypho
quasi leo in spelunca sua; insidiatur, ut rapiat pauperem.
Ascensio enim Esaiae et Apocalypsis Eliae hoc habent testimonium.

Jerome has substituted for the Roman Psalter's in occulto)
like a lion in his cave, he lies in ambush to seize the poor"
(Ps 10:9). For the Ascension of Isaiah and the Apocalypse of
Elijah contain this quotation.

[Jerome, Commentary on Isaiah, Bk 17, on 64:4]

T7. Let us go on to the Apostle Paul. He writes to the Corinthians "For if they had known, they would never have cruci-
fied the Lord of Glory. But as it is written, 'What eye has
not seen, nor ear heard, nor have they gone up into the heart of
man'"... In this passage some people usually look for the rav-
ings of Apocryphal works, and say that the quotation has been
taken from the Apocalypse of Elijah, although in Isaiah, according to the Hebrew text, it may be read in this form "From
everlasting they have not heard, nor with their ears perceived.
Eye has not seen, O God, apart from Thee, the things Thou hast
prepared for those who wait for Thee" (Isa 64:4). The Septua-
gint translated this very differently. "From everlasting we
have not heard nor have our eyes seen, a God apart from Thee,
nor Thy true works, and Thou shalt work mercy for those who
wait for Thee." We understand from where he took the quotation, but the Apostle did not render it word for word, but in
a paraphrastic manner he indicated the same sense with different words.

[Jerome, Epistle LVII (quondam 101) to Pammachius]

4.5, 1 perciperunt E, corr.   6 oculis nostris E, corr.
6 uidebunt deus E   10 epistolam E   ·12 contendit E
12 utitur] auditur praem. E, sed del.

S. Hieronymi Opera I 2A ed. M. Adriaen (Corpus Christianorum 73A;
Turnholti: Brepols, 1963) 735 = P.L. 24.622

10 Pergamus ad apostolum Paulum. Scribit ad Corinthios: "Si
    enim cognouissent, numquam Dominum maiestatis crucifixissent.
    Sed, sicut scriptum est: quod oculus non uidit nec auris
    audiuit nec in cor hominis ascenderunt, quae praeparauit Deus
15 diligentibus se". Solent in hoc loco apocryphorum quidam
    deliramenta sectari, et dicere quod de Apocalypsi Heliae
    testimonium sumptum sit, cum in Isaia iuxta Hebraicum ita
    legatur: "a saeculo non audierunt neque auribus perceperunt.
20 Oculus non uidit, Deus, absque te, quae praeparasti expectan-
    tibus te". Hoc Septuaginta multo aliter transtulerunt: "a
    saeculo non audiuimus, neque oculi nostri uiderunt Deum
    absque te, et opera tua uera, et facies expectantibus te
25 misericordiam". Intellegimus unde sumpsit testimonium, et
    tamen Apostolus non uerbum expressit e uerbo, sed παραφρασ-
    τικῶς eundem sensum aliis sermonibus indicauit.

    11 I Cor. 2:8-9 | 18 Isai. LXIV 4 (sec. Hebr.) | 21 Isai.
    LXIV 4 (sec. LXX) |
    13 quod] quae ΩΣDS | 15 hoc] isto ΩΣDS | 24 uera et sic
    codd. omnes.

S. Jérome, Lettres, III, ed. J. Labourt (Collection Budé; Paris:
Les Belles Lettres, 1953) 68.

IIIa T8. Perhaps Hegesippus, who is credited with denying the canonical status of a statement virtually equivalent with 1 Cor 2:9,
should be considered a supporter of its apocryphal nature:

> (Gobarus said) that <u>the good things prepared for the righteous</u>
>
> <u>neither eye saw nor ear heard nor did they come up into the</u>
>
> <u>heart of men</u>. But Hegesippus, a man of long ago, and of the
>
> time of the Apostles, in the fifth book of his Memoirs says --
>
> I don't know what led him to do so -- that these things were
>
> said vainly, and that those who said them lied both against
>
> the divine Scriptures and the Lord who said, "Blessed are
>
> your eyes for they see, and your ears for they hear, etc."
>
> (Matt 13:6).
>
> [Hegesippus, quoted by Stephen Gobarus, quoted by Photius,
>
> <u>Bibliotheca</u>, Codex 232.]

"Οτι τὰ ἡτοιμασμένα τοῖς δικαίοις ἀγαθὰ οὔτε ὀφθαλμὸς εἶδεν

10 οὔτε οὖς ἤκουσεν οὔτε ἐπὶ καρδίαν ἀνθρώπου ἀνέβη. Ἡγήσιππος

μέντοι, ἀρχαῖός τε ἀνὴρ καὶ ἀποστολικός, ἐν τῷ πέμπτῳ τῶν

ὑπομνημάτων, οὐκ οἶδ' ὅ τι καὶ παθών, μάτην μὲν εἰρῆσθαι

ταῦτα λέγει, καὶ καταψεύδεσθαι τοὺς ταῦτα φαμένους τῶν τε

15 θείων γραφῶν καὶ τοῦ Κυρίου λέγοντος· "Μακάριοι οἱ ὀφθαλμοὶ

ὑμῶν οἱ βλέποντες καὶ τὰ ὦτα ὑμῶν τὰ ἀκούοντα" καὶ ἑξῆς.

Photius, Bibliothèque, V (Collection Byzance-Budé; Paris: Les
Belles Lettres, 1967) 70 (ed. R. Henry)

Fragment IV

"AWAKE, O SLEEPER"

Fragment IV "Awake, O sleeper"

IVa   Quoted as scripture.

Therefore it says, "Awake, O Sleeper, and arise from the dead,

and [a]Christ will shine upon you[a]".'

[Ephesians 5:14]

Variant a-a: "Christ will lay hand upon you" or "you shall

lay hold of Christ."

The quotation is discussed in A. Resch, Agrapha; aussercanonische
Schriftfragmente[2] (Texte und Untersuchungen NF XV 3-4; Leipzig:
1906) 32-4, and Register ad loc., and by most commentaries on Eph
ad loc.

IVa T1. The first ascription is to Elijah [or Isaiah (ΗΛΙΑC <
ΗCΑΙΑC) cf. K. Holl's note in his edition of this text, and cf.IVc].
            Scholion 2 (on Ephesians) = 37 (on the Pauline Corpus):

Therefore it says, Awake, O Sleeper, and arise from the dead,

and Christ will shine upon you.

Refutation 2 (On Ephesians) = 37 (on the Pauline Corpus):

From where did the Apostle get the passage "Therefore it says,

etc.", except obviously from the Old Testament: and this pas-

sage is found in Elijah(?). And from where did Elijah take

his point of departure? He was one of those Prophets who

lived according to the Law, and he took his point of departure

from the Law and the Prophets. If he prophesied in Christ

"Awake, O Sleeper, and arise from the dead, and Christ will

shine upon you" then the Prototype had been fulfilled through

Lazarus and the others: about him his followers had doubts,

Mary and Martha saying,"He stinks already,for he is four days

dead."(Jn 11:.9),those of the ruler of the Synagogue say,"Do not

14 διὸ λέγει· ἔγειρε ὁ καθεύδων καὶ ἀνάστα ἐκ τῶν νεκρῶν,

καὶ   ἐπιφαύσει σοι ὁ Χριστός.

14 ἔγειραι H^{δ}48 |a^3 216 205 b1 253 2δ309 209f   ua | ἐπιφαύσεις
τοῦ Χ͞Υ |a^1 1026* Χρ θδτ Or Vict Ambrst

H. von Soden, op. cit. (IIIa, supra.) 769

25   B͞ καὶ λ͞ζ σχόλιον. "Διὸ λέγει· ἔγειρε ὁ καθεύδων καὶ
ἀνάστα ἐκ τῶν νεκρῶν καὶ ἐπιφαύσει σοι ὁ Χριστός".

B͞ καὶ λ͞ζ ἔλεγχος. Πόθεν τῷ ἀποστόλῳ τὸ "διὸ λέγει"

1 ἀλλὰ ἀπὸ τῆς παλαιᾶς δῆλον διαθήκης; τοῦτο δὲ ἐμφέρεται παρὰ
τῷ Ἠλίᾳ. πόθεν δὲ ὡρμᾶτο ὁ Ἠλίας; ἀλλὰ εἷς ἦν τῶν προφητῶν
τῶν κατὰ νόμον πεπολιτευμένων, ἀπὸ νόμου καὶ προφητῶν
ὁρμώμενος. εἰ δὲ ἐν Χριστῷ ἐπροφήτευσε τὸ "ἔγειρε ὁ καθεύδων

5 καὶ ἀνάστα ἐκ τῶν νεκρῶν καὶ ἐπιφαύσει σοι ὁ Χριστός", ἄρα
γε τὸ πρωτότυπον διὰ Λαζάρου καὶ τῶν ἄλλων ἐπεπλήρωτο, περὶ
οὗ οἱ αὐτοὶ ἀμφέβαλλον, Μάρθα καὶ Μαρία λέγουσαι "ἤδη ὄζει,
τεταρταῖός ἐστι" καὶ τῶν τοῦ ἀρχισυναγώγου λεγόντων "μηκέτι
σκύλλετε τὸν διδάσκαλον" καὶ αὐτοῦ λέγοντος "μὴ φοβεῖσθε·
οὐ γὰρ ἀπέθανεν, ἀλλὰ καθεύδει".

25f καὶ ἀνάστα ἐκ νεκρῶν < S. 119, 11 26 καὶ < S. 119, 11
27 after διὸ + καὶ M eras V corr   2 ὁρμᾶται V   3 before
νόμου + τοῦ M   4 προεφήτευσεν from ἐπροφήτευσεν V corr
προεφήτευε M   6 περὶ οὗ *] περὶ ὧν VM

trouble the Teacher any more," (Luke 8:49) and He himself saying,"Don't be afraid, she is not dead, but asleep." (Luke 8:53).

[Epiphanius, Panarion Haer. 42.12.3, Refutation 37 against
Marcion]

IVa T2a Ascribed to "the Apocryphon of Jeremiah."
In the letter to the Ephesians there are six divine testi-
monies: one from Genesis, the fifth in order; one from Deuteronomy, the sixth in order; one from Psalm 4, the third in
order; one from Psalm 67 (68), the second in order; one from
the Prophet Isaiah, the first in order; and one from the
Apocryphon of Jeremiah, the fourth in order.

[Euthalius Diaconus, Prolog. in XIV S. Pauli Ap. epistolas]

IVa T2b Here too, Euthalius is followed by Photius, Quaestiones
ad Amphilochium, 151; cf. IIIa T3b.
But also in the epistle to the Ephesians, "Rise....give you
light" is from the apocrypha said to be by Jeremiah.

IVa T3 Ascribed to the "so-called Apocrypha of Jeremiah" or
"the apocrypha said to be by Jeremiah," by George the Syncellus

But even the blessed Paul made sparing use of certain passages
from the Apocrypha: thus, when he says in the first Epistle to
the Corinthians "What eye saw not, nor did ear hear, nor did
they come into the heart of man, etc." this is from the
Apocrypha of Elijah, and again "Neither is circumcision any-
thing, nor uncircumcision, but a new creation" in the Letter
to the Galatians is from the Apocalypse of Moses, and "Awake,
O Sleeper, and arise from the dead, and Christ will shine upon

K. Holl (ed.), Epiphanius, II (GCS 31; Leipzig: Hinrichs, 1922) 179-180, cf. p. 119; Migne, PG 41.807

Ἐν τῇ πρὸς Ἐφεσίους ἐπιστολῇ ϛ'· Γενέσεως Ι· ε'.
Δευτερονομίου Ι· ϛ'. Ψαλμοῦ τετάρτου Ι· γ'. Ψαλμοῦ ξζ', Ι·
β'. Ἡσαΐου προφήτου Ι· α'. Ἰερεμίου ἀποκρύφου Ι· δ'.

Migne, P.G. 85.721

ἀλλὰ καὶ ἐν τῇ πρὸς Ἐφεσίους ἐκ τῶν λεγομένων Ἰερεμίου
ἀποκρύφων· ἔγειραι ὁ καθεύδων . . . Χριστός.

Migne, P.G. 101.813.

πλὴν καὶ ὁ μακάριος Παῦλος σπανίως ἐχρήσατό τισιν ἐξ
ἀποκρύφων χρήσεσιν, ὡς ὅταν φησὶν ἐν τῇ πρὸς Κορινθίους
πρώτη ἐπιστολῇ "ἃ ὀφθαλμὸς οὐκ εἶδε καὶ οὖς οὐκ ἤκουσε καὶ
5 ἐπὶ καρδίαν ἀνθρώπου οὐκ ἀνέβη" καὶ τὰ ἑξῆς Ἠλία ἀποκρύφων.
καὶ πάλιν ἐν τῇ πρὸς Γαλάτας ἐκ τῆς Μωϋσέως ἀποκαλύψεως
"οὔτε περιτομή τι ἐστιν οὔτε ἀκροβυστία, ἀλλὰ καινὴ κτίσις."
καὶ ἐν τῇ πρὸς Ἐφεσίους ἐκ τῶν Ἰερεμίου λεγομένων ἀποκρύφων
"ἔγειραι ὁ καθεύδων καὶ ἀνάστα ἐκ τῶν νεκρῶν, καὶ ἐπιφαύσει
σοι ὁ Χριστός."

4 εἶδεν A   οἶδεν G   6 Διὰ τί ἔνια (ἔνια G εἶναι A) ἀπόβλητα

you'' in Ephesians is from the so-called <u>Apocrypha of Jeremiah</u>.

IVa   T4   The same attribution is made in marginal notes to some
MSS of the Epistles (cf. Resch, <u>Agrapha</u>... p. 33).

IVb   Ascribed to Isaiah (or Elijah, i.e. ΗΛΙΑϹ > ΗϹΑΙΑϹ? cf. IVa T1)

And Isaiah says 'Awake, O Sleeper, and arise from the dead,

and Christ will shine upon you.'

[Hippolytus, <u>Commentary on Daniel</u>, 4.56.4]

IVc   Ascribed to ''a prophet'' (by the same writer who makes the
attribution to Elijah [or Isaiah] in IVb).

And the prophet says Awake, o Sleeper, and arise from the dead,

and Christ will shine upon you.

[Hippolytus,<u>On Christ and Anti-christ</u>, LXV]

On this fragment (IVa or IVa-c) cf. A. Oepke s.v. κρύπτω, <u>TDNT</u>,
III, p. 990, E. Schürer <u>Geschichte</u>..., III, p. 362. If this be-
longs to the same Elianic work as the other fgg. can it have been
other than Christian?

νόθια margo A   6 Γαλάτας] V, 6 τῆς] τοῦ m.   7 ἐστὶν A
ἔσται G   8 Ἐφεσίους] V | τῶν A τοῦ G.

Georgius Syncellus in Chronographia. Georgius Syncellus et Nicephorus Cp. ed. Dindorf (Corpus Scriptorum Historiae Byzantinae 1;
Bonn: E. Weber, 1829) 48.

4 καὶ Ἡσαΐας λέγει· "ἔγειρε ὁ καθεύ|δων καὶ ἐξεγέρθητι ἐκ

τῶν νεκρῶν, καὶ ἐπιφαύσει σοι ὁ Χριστός".

καὶ] ὡς S: ὁ + B | ἡσαΐας A | ἔγειρε -- Χριστός] Ant 65
S. 35, 2. Refut. V, 7 S. 146, 76 | ἐγείραι Ge | ἐξηγέρθητι
A: ἀνάστα B cf. Eph. 5, 14 |

G.N. Bonwetsch (ed.), Hippolytus I.i (GCS 1; Leipzig: J.C. Hinrichs,
1897) p. 328; M. Lefèvre, Hippolyte Commentaire sur Daniel (Sources
Chrétiennes 14; Paris: Ed. du Cerf. 1947) 376

ὁ δὲ προφήτης λέγει· "ἔγειρε ὁ καθεύδων καὶ ἐξεγέρθητι ἐκ

τῶν νεκρῶν, καὶ ἐπιφαύσει σοι ὁ Χριστός."

ἔγειρε HERS | καὶ < S |

PG, 10.785A; H. Achelis, Hippolytus I.ii (GCS 1; Leipzig: Hinrichs,
1897) p. 45

Fragment V

ON THE ANTICHRIST

Fragment V. On the Antichrist

The following adespoton was hesitantly ascribed to the Elijah
Apocryphon by M.R. James on the grounds of the form of the quotation, and its contents op. cit. (Introduction, supra) 92; see
also Denis, op. cit.(Introduction, supra) 165, 298.

> Va. And another prophet (i.e. other than Jeremiah) also says,
> "He will gather together all his power from the rising of the
> sun to the setting of the sun; those whom he has called and
> those whom he has not called will go with him; he will make
> the sea white with the sails of his ships, and the land black
> with shields and weapons; and everyone who will meet him in
> battle will fall by the sword."
> [Hippolytus, On Christ and Antichrist 15]

> Vb. For he will summon all the people to himself, from every
> region of the diaspora, adopting them as his own children,
> promising that he will restore their land and raise up their
> kingship and temple, in order that he may be worshipped by
> them as God: as the prophet says, "He will gather together all
> his power, from the rising of the sun to the setting of the
> sun; those whom he has called and those whom he has not called
> will go with him."
> [Hippolytus, On Christ and Antichrist 54]

λέγει δὲ καὶ ἕτερος προφήτης· "συνάξει[1] πᾶσαν δύναμιν αὐτοῦ

ἀπὸ ἡλίου ἀνατολῶν μέχρις[3] ἡλίου[2] δυσμῶν· οὓς κεκλήκει

καὶ οὓς οὐ κεκλήκει πορεύ/σονται[4] μετ' αὐτοῦ· λευκανεῖ τὴν

θάλασσαν ἀπὸ τῶν ἱστίων τῶν πλοίων   αὐτοῦ[5] καὶ[6] μελανεῖ τὸ

πεδίον ἀπὸ τῶν θυρεῶν καὶ τῶν ὅπλων· καὶ πᾶς   ὃς ἂν

συναντήσει[7] αὐτῷ ἐν πολέμῳ, ἐν[8] μαχαίρᾳ[9] πεσεῖται."

1 συνάξει HE, ξυνάξει R   2 < Slav   3 μέχρις H,
ἄχρις ER   4 πορεύσονται HE, πορευθήσονται R   5 αὐτοῦ
< ER   6 < ER   7 συναντήσει H, συναντήσῃ ER .   8< ER   9
μαχαίρᾳ ER, μαχαίρῃ H

Achelis (ed.), op. cit. (IVc, supra.) 12 = P.G. 10.740

οὗτος[1] γὰρ προσκαλέσεται   πάντα   τὸν λαὸν πρὸς ἑαυτὸν ἐκ

πάσης χώρας τῆς διασπορᾶς, ἰδιο/ποιούμενος αὐτοὺς[2] ὡς ἴδια

τέκνα[3], ἐπαγγελλόμενος[4] αὐτοῖς[5] ἀποκατα/στήσειν τὴν χώραν

καὶ ἀναστήσειν αὐτῶν τὴν βασιλείαν   καὶ τὸν   ναόν,[5'] ἵνα

ὑπ' αὐτῶν ὡς θεὸς προσκυνηθῇ, ὡς λέγει ὁ προφήτης·

"συνάξει πᾶσαν αὐτοῦ τὴν δύναμιν[6] ἀπὸ ἡλίου ἀνατολῶν[7]

ἄχρι ἡλίου[8]   δυσμῶν, οὓς κεκλήκει καὶ οὓς οὐ κεκλήκει

πορεύσονται μετ' αὐτοῦ."

1 οὗτος H, αὐτὸς ER   2 αὐτοὺς < ER   3 ἴδια τέκνα H,
τέκνα ἴδια ER   4 ἐπαγγελόμενος E   5 αὐτοῖς < ER   5'
ναόν HS, λαόν ER   6 αὐτοῦ τὴν δύναμιν HS, τὴν βασιλείαν
αὐτοῦ ER   7 ἡλίου ἀνατολῶν H, ἀνατολῶν ἡλίου ER   8< ERS

Ibid., 36; = P.G. 10.773.

Fragment VI

ELIJAH AND LILITH

Fragment VI.   Elijah and Lilith

> And thus run their (i.e. the Gnostics') frivolous and fanci-
> ful stories, how they even make bold to blaspheme about the
> holy Elijah, and to claim that a story tells how, when he
> had been taken up, he was cast back into the world. For, it
> says, a female demon came and laid hold upon him, and said
> to him, "Where are you going? For I have children from you,
> and you can't go up into heaven and leave your children here."
> And he said -- so the story goes -- "How do you have children
> from me? For I was always chaste." The demon says (according
> to this book), "But I do! When you were dreaming dreams, you
> often were voided by an emission from the body; and I was the
> one who took up the seeds from you, and begot you children."
> Vast is the stupidity of those who say this sort of thing.
>
> [Epiphanius,Panarion, Haer. 26 13.228 (against the Gnostics)]

Whether this gnostic tale was found in the same work as the pre-
ceding fragments is not certain; it might have derived from independent Gnostic tradition, or even a distinct Gnostic Apocalypse/
Ascension/ of Elijah.

4 καὶ οὕτως[1]ἐστὶ τὰ ληρώδη αὐτῶν καὶ μυθώδη,[2] ὡς καὶ περὶ

τοῦ ἁγίου Ἠλία τολμῶσι βλασφημεῖν καὶ λέγειν ὅτι, φησίν, ὅτε

ἀνελήφθη, κατεβλήθη πάλιν εἰς τὸν κόσμον. 5 ἦλθεν γάρ,

φησίν, μία δαίμων καὶ ἐκράτησε καὶ εἶπεν αὐτῷ ὅτι ποῦ πορεύῃ;

ἔχω γὰρ τέκνα ἀπὸ σοῦ, καὶ οὐ δύνασαι ἀνελθεῖν καὶ ὧδε ἀφεῖναι

τὰ τέκνα σου. καί, φησίν, λέγει· πόθεν ἔχεις τέκνα ἀπ' ἐμοῦ

καὶ ἐγὼ ἤμην ἐν ἁγνείᾳ; λέγει, φησίν· ναί, ὅτε ἐνυπνίοις[3]

ἐνυπνιαζόμενος πολλάκις ἐν τῇ ἀπορροίᾳ τῶν σωμάτων ἐκενώθης,

ἐγὼ ἤμην ἡ μεταλαβοῦσα ἀπὸ σοῦ τὰ σπέρματα καὶ γεννῶσά σοι[4]

υἱούς. 6 πολλὴ δὲ μωρία τῶν τὰ τοιαῦτα λεγόντων.

1 οὕτως] ταῦτα, V.corr 1-2 perhaps read ἐστὶ <κτηνώδη> τὰ
ληρώδη αὐτῶν μυθολογήματα* 3 ἐνύπνοις M 4 γεννῶσά σοι]
γεννῶσας M; γεννήσασά σοι? Jül.

K. Holl (ed.), Epiphanius, Ancoratus u. Panarion 1 (GCS 25; Leipzig: J.C. Hinrichs, 1915) 293.

PART   2

THE VITA ELIAE and THE SHORT HISTORY

OF ELIJAH THE PROPHET

1. THE VITA ELIAE

The text of Vitae Prophetarum dealing with Elijah is quoted
from Th. Schermann, Prophetarum Vitae Fabulosae Indices Apostolorum
Discipulorumque Domini Dorotheo Epiphanio Hippolyto aliisque vindi-
cata (Leipzig: Teubner, 1907). The four recensions printed there
appear on pp. 6-7 (Epiphanii Prior), 52-3 (Dorothei), 66-7 (Epiphanii Altera), and 93-4 (Anonyma). See for a diplomatic text of MS Q
(Cod. Marchal.) of the last of these: Charles C. Torrey, The Lives
of the Prophets (J.B.L. Monograph Series I; Philadelphia: S.B.L.
1946) 32 (text) and 47 (translation). The text of Rec. Anon., gen-
erally considered to be superior, is followed, but only the first
part is here given = (A) (Schermann, p. 93 ll. 7-14), since what
follows is merely a summary of the biblical narrative concerning
Elijah. Significant variants of the other recensions are noted.

Following this, the first paragraph of Dorothei Recensio is
given (B), since it contains interesting additional traditions
(Schermann, p. 52, ll. 10-23). Then follows the conclusion of
Epiphanii Recensio Altera (C), which again presents material of
interest (Schermann, p. 67, ll. 5-13).

A

7   Elijah was a Tishbite from the land of the Arabs, of the tribe of

8   Aaron, dwelling /in Gilead, for Tishbi was a gift for the pries-

9   ts. When he was /to be born, his father Sobacha saw that white

10,11   /shining men called him by name and that they swa/ddled him in

12   fire and gave him a flame of fire to eat. He went and/reported

13   this in Jerusalem and the oracle said to him, "Do not / fear,

     for his dwelling will be light and his word / decision and he

     will judge Israel."

                                                        8 gift]
     dwelling Ep Pr Dor Ep Al An E   9 father] mother Ep Al An E
     11 he went] his father Asōm went Ep Al   12 reported] + to
     the priests Ep Pr   14 decision]+and his life (+ with the
     angels An E) with the winged creatures and his zeal pleasing
     (+ before the Lord AnBB^1) AnBB^{1}E   14 Israel] + with sword
     and with fire Ep Pr Dor Ep Al An BB^{1}EF + and he will be taken
     up in a shaking from the heavens An BB^{1}F
     [Vitae Prophetarum, Recensio Anonyma]

                              B

                         On Elijah

     He is Elijah the first one of men who demonstrated running

     through the sky to men, the[†]first of men who showed[†]who had

     a sharè of the earth as a dwelling and ran through the whole

     heavens; who was mortal and contended with the immortal ones;

     who walked upon the earth and as a spirit traversed the

     heavens with angels; who, through the sheepskin gave double

     gifts to his disciple Elisha; the long-lived and unaging

7,8 Ἡλίας θεσβίτης ἐκ γῆς Ἀράβων,φυλῆς Ἀαρών, οἰκῶν / ἐν Γαλαάδ

9 ὅτι ἡ Θέσβις δόμα ἦν τοῖς ἱερεῦσιν. Ὅτε εἶχε /τεχθῆναι, εἶδε

10 Σοβαχὰ ὁ πατὴρ αὐτοῦ, ὅτι ἄνδρες λευκο-/φανεῖς αὐτὸν

11 προσηγόρευον, καὶ ὅτι ἐν πυρὶ αὐτὸν ἐσπαρ-/γάνουν, καὶ

12 φλόγα πυρὸς ἐδίδουν αὐτῷ φαγεῖν καὶ ἐλθὼν / ἀνήγγειλεν

13 ἐν Ἱερουσαλὴμ καὶ εἶπεν αὐτῷ ὁ χρησμός· μὴ / δειλιάσῃς·

14 ἔσται γὰρ ἡ οἴκησις αὐτοῦ φῶς καὶ ὁ λόγος αὐτοῦ / ἀπόφασις
καὶ κρινεῖ τὸν Ἰσραήλ.

8 δόμα] δῶμα
Ep Pr Dor Ep Al   9 πατήρ] μήτηρ Ep Al An E   11 ἐλθὼν] +
ὁ πατὴρ αὐτοῦ Ἀσωμ Ep Al   12 ἀνήγγειλεν] + τοῖς ἱερεῦσιν
Ep Pr   14 ἀπόφασις] + καὶ ἡ ζωὴ αὐτοῦ (+ μετ' ἀγγέλων E)
μετὰ τῶν πετηνῶν καὶ ὁ ζῆλος αὐτοῦ ἀρεστὸς (+ ἐνώπιον κυρίου
BB[1]) An BB[1]E   14 Ἰσραήλ] + ἐν ῥομφαίᾳ καὶ ἐν πυρὶ Ep Pr
Dor etc. +καὶ ἀναληφθήσεται ἐν συσσεισμῷ ἐκ τῶν οὐρανῶν An
BB[1]F.

Th. Schermann, Proph. Vit. Fab. etc. 93, ll. 7-14.

Εἰς τὸν Ἡλίαν

Οὗτός ἐστιν Ἡλίας ὁ πρῶτος ἀνθρώπων τοῖς ἀνθρώποις
ὑποδείξας οὐρανοδραμεῖν,[+]ὁ πρῶτος ἀνθρώπων ὑποδείξας[+]ὁ τὴν
γῆν λαχὼν οἰκητήριον καὶ τὸν οὐρανὸν ἀθρόον διατρέχων, ὁ
θνητὸς ὑπάρχων καὶ τοῖς ἀθανάτοις ἁμιλλώμενος, ὁ χαμαὶ
βαδίζων καὶ ὡς πνεῦμα μετ' ἀγγέλων οὐρανοπολῶν· ὁ διὰ τῆς
μηλωτῆς τῷ μαθητῇ Ἐλισσαίῳ διπλᾶ τὰ χαρίσματα μεταδούς·
ὁ μακροχρόνιος καὶ ἀγήρως ἄνθρωπος, ὁ τῷ Ἀντίχριστῳ

man, preserved as general against the Anti-Christ, who is set up
against and exposes his deceit and pride, who turns all men
from his error to God in the end. He is the one who is
reckoned worthy to be the forerunner of the second and manifest coming of the Lord Christ who by measure of his
services contends with the angels.

[Vitae Prophetarum, Dorothei Recensio]

C

For having been a zealot and strict guardian of the command-
ments of God and having been reckoned worthy of the greatest
mysteries and divine oracles, he was taken up in a fiery
chariot. He will again come before the end as God said
through Malachi, "Behold I will send you Elijah the Tishbite
before the coming of the great and manifest day of the Lord,
who shall turn the father's heart to the son and each man's
heart to his neighbour, lest I come and smite the earth
utterly." (Mal 4:5-6)

[Vitae Prophetarum, Epiphanii Recensio Altera]

διατηρούμενος στρατηγός, ὁ ἀντικαθιστάμενος καὶ διελέγχων

τὴν ἀπάτην καὶ τὴν ὑπερηφανίαν αὐτοῦ, ὁ πάντας ἀνθρώπους

ἐκ τῆς πλάνης αὐτοῦ ἐπὶ τὸν θεὸν ἐν τῇ συντελείᾳ ἐπιστρέφων·

οὗτος ὁ τῆς δευτέρας καὶ ἐπιφανοῦς παρουσίας τοῦ δεσπότου

Χριστοῦ ἀξιούμενος εἶναι πρόδρομος ὁ μέτρῳ διακονιῶν τοῖς

ἀγγέλοις ἁμιλλώμενος.

Th. Schermann, Prophet. Vit. Fab. etc., 52, 11. 10-20.

Καὶ γὰρ ζηλωτὴς καὶ φύλαξ τῶν τοῦ θεοῦ ἐντολῶν ἀκριβὴς

γεγονὼς καὶ μεγίστων μυστηρίων καὶ χαρισμάτων θείων ἀξιωθεὶς

ἀνελήφθη ἐν ἅρματι πυρίνῳ, ὃς πάλιν ἐλεύσεται πρὸ τῆς

συντελείας, ὥς φησιν ὁ θεὸς διὰ Μαλαχίου· ἰδοὺ ἐξαποστελῶ

ὑμῖν Ἠλίαν τὸν Θεσβίτην πρὶν ἐλθεῖν τὴν ἡμέραν κυρίου τὴν

μεγάλην καὶ ἐπιφανῆ, ὃς ἀποκαταστήσει καρδίαν πατρὸς πρὸς

υἱόν, καὶ καρδίαν ἀνθρώπου πρὸς τὸν πλησίον αὐτοῦ· μὴ ἐλθὼν

πατάξω τὴν γῆν ἄρδην.

Th. Schermann, Prophet. Vit. Fab. 67, 11. 5-13.

98

2. The Short History of Elijah the Prophet

This work was published by S. Yovsēp'ianc', Ankanon Girk'
Hin Ktakaranac' [Uncanonical Books of the Old Testament], (Venice:
Mechitarist Press 1896) 333-342. His edition was based on one
MS: Venice, Mechitarist Library No. 1541, written in 1627 C.E.
The work was translated into English by J. Issaverdens, Uncanon-
ical Writings of the Old Testament (Venice: Mechitarist Press,
2 ed. 1934) 172-191. A study of it in Armenian is to be found
in B. Sargissian, Usumnasirut'iwnk' Hin Ktakarani Anvawer Groc'
Vray [Studies on the Apocryphal Writings of the Old Testament]
(Venice: Mechitarist Press, 1889) 273-279. Notice was also taken
of the book by M.R. James, Apocrypha Anecdota II (Texts and Studies V 1; Cambridge: Cambridge University Press, 1897) 164.

Numerous additional manuscripts exist. Among the catalogued
manuscripts in the Patriarchal Library in Jerusalem copies are
found in: No. 393, notragir; No. 631 (XVII saec.) -- this copy
contains 17 pages of text in addition to that published by
Yovsēp'ianc'; No. 669 (1694 C.E.); No. 694 (1596 C.E.); No. 730
notragir; No. 876, notragir; No. 1012, bolorgir; No. 1047; No. 1434
(17th century); No. 1623, notragir; No. 1861 (1669 C.E.) containing 24 additional pages. On these see: N. Bogharian, Grand Catalogue of St. James Manuscripts I-VI (Jerusalem: St. James Press,
1966-1972) [in Armenian]. In the Institute for Ancient Manuscripts
in Erevan, Armenia, two copies are found with the same title,
No. 503 (1601 C.E.) and No. 4355 (XVIII saec.). The Catalogue
of that Library gives no incipits, so it is more than likely that
most, if not all the works recorded under the slightly differing
title History of Elijah the Prophet are identical with the Short
History of Elijah the Prophet. These occur in No. 701 (1730 C.E.);
No.706 (XVII saec.); No. 2131 (XVII saec.); 2168 (XVII saec.);
2196 (XVII saec.); 2242 (XVII saec.); 2245 (1689 C.E.); 2252 (XVII
saec.); 3237 (XVII saec.); 3350 (XVIII saec.); 6092 (XVII saec.);
6995 (XVII, XVIII saec.); 8239 (1615 C.E.); 9289 (1592 C.E.).

The same may also be true of the work entitled <u>Concerning Elijah</u> <u>the Prophet</u> in No. 8093 (XVIII saec.). See: O. Eganyan, A. Zeyt'unyan and P. Ant'abyan, <u>C'uc'ak Jeragrac' Maštoc'i Anvan</u> <u>Matenadarani</u> [<u>Catalogue of the Manuscripts of the Mastoc' Library</u>], I-II (Erevan: Armenian Academy of Sciences, 1965-1970). Doubtless further copies could be listed from other collections.

The book opens with an extract from the <u>Vita Eliae</u> in the <u>Vitae Prophetarum</u> in a form not identical with the Armenian version of that Vita.[1] There follow various narratives based on the biblical Elijah stories. <u>Inter alia</u> the following points are noteworthy. The child of the widow, whom Elijah raised from death (I Ki. 17) is identified with Jonah, as in other Armenian sources and also in Jewish traditions, such as <u>j. Succah</u> 5.1 (55a), <u>Mid. Teh.</u> (ed. Buber) 26, p. 220. The Obadiah of 1 Kings 18, who is referred to in <u>The Short History of Elijah the Prophet</u> is not identified in this work with the prophet of the same name, as was done in the <u>Vita Obadiae</u>, Rabbinic sources such as <u>Sifré Bamidbar</u> (ed. Horovitz) p. 133, p. 176, and <u>b. Sanh.</u> 39b. Cf. also Jerome on <u>Obad</u> 1 (Migne, P.L., 25.1099).

The incident with the priests of Baal is much developed. Most characteristic is the story of how the priests hid a man under the altar to set fire to their wood. This tradition was already remarked upon by James (<u>op. cit.</u>). The plot is foiled by Elijah whose prayer to God results in the man's death. The book, as published, opens with the imposition of the drought in response to Elijah's prayer. It concludes rather abruptly with the coming of the rain and "Ahab wept and went to his home."

The book is Christian in authorship. In particular it is comparable to the Armenian apocryphal works of the type called "Biblical Paraphrases" which contain a paraphrase of Biblical narrative texts, expanded with apocryphal traditions on the one hand and passages of typological Christian exegesis on the other.[2] One such passage is to be observed in the present work, that which

1. This latter is to appear in Michael E. Stone, <u>Armenian Apocrypha</u> <u>relating to Patriarchs and Prophets</u> (Jerusalem: Israel Academy of Sciences, in press).
2. Extensive texts of this type will be published in Stone, <u>ibid.</u>

draws the parallel between the unclean raven passing over the
Jordan to bring Elijah food and the heathen passing through the
waters of baptism by which they were cleansed. Other features
of the story too are unmistakably Christian. Yet, as we have
shown above, many of the traditions are very ancient with clear
parallels in early Jewish sources.

COMPREHENSIVE INDEX

COMPREHENSIVE INDEX

This index includes citations of ancient sources as well as
references to ancient persons and places. It does not include
modern authors.